W9-CND-909

Cybercrime

Other Books in the Current Controversies Series

Cybercrime

Noël Merino, Book Editor

GREENHAVEN PRESS
A part of Gale, Cengage Learning

GALE
CENGAGE Learning·

Farmington Hills, Mich • San Francisco • New York • Waterville, Maine
Meriden, Conn • Mason, Ohio • Chicago

GALE
CENGAGE Learning

Judy Galens, *Manager, Frontlist Acquisitions*

For more information, contact:
Greenhaven Press
27500 Drake Rd.
Farmington Hills, MI 48331-3535
Or you can visit our Internet site at gale.cengage.com

Articles in Greenhaven Press anthologies are often edited for length to meet page requirements. In addition, original titles of these works are changed to clearly present the main thesis and to explicitly indicate the author's opinion. Every effort is made to ensure that Greenhaven Press accurately reflects the original intent of the authors. Every effort has been made to trace the owners of copyrighted material.

LIBRARY OF CONGRESS CATALOGING-IN-PUBLICATION DATA

Cybercrime (Greenhaven Press)
  Cybercrime / Noël Merino, book editor.
    pages cm. -- (Current controversies)
  Includes bibliographical references and index.
  ISBN 978-0-7377-7420-7 (hardcover) -- ISBN 978-0-7377-7421-4 (pbk.)
  1. Computer crimes. I. Merino, Noël, editor. II. Title.
  HV6773.C918 2016
  364.16'8--dc23
                          2015026912

Printed in the United States of America
  1 2 3 4 5   20 19 18 17 16

Contents

Chapter 3: How Should US Cybersecurity Be Improved?

Chapter 4: What Should Be Done to Protect Internet Users from Cybercrime?

Foreword

By definition, controversies are "discussions of questions in which opposing opinions clash" (*Webster's Twentieth Century Dictionary Unabridged*). Few would deny that controversies are a pervasive part of the human condition and exist on virtually every level of human enterprise. Controversies transpire between individuals and among groups, within nations and between nations. Controversies supply the grist necessary for progress by providing challenges and challengers to the status quo. They also create atmospheres where strife and warfare can flourish. A world without controversies would be a peaceful world; but it also would be, by and large, static and prosaic.

The Series' Purpose

The purpose of the Current Controversies series is to explore many of the social, political, and economic controversies dominating the national and international scenes today. Titles selected for inclusion in the series are highly focused and specific. For example, from the larger category of criminal justice, Current Controversies deals with specific topics such as police brutality, gun control, white collar crime, and others. The debates in Current Controversies also are presented in a useful, timeless fashion. Articles and book excerpts included in each title are selected if they contribute valuable, long-range ideas to the overall debate. And wherever possible, current information is enhanced with historical documents and other relevant materials. Thus, while individual titles are current in focus, every effort is made to ensure that they will not become quickly outdated. Books in the Current Controversies series will remain important resources for librarians, teachers, and students for many years.

In addition to keeping the titles focused and specific, great care is taken in the editorial format of each book in the series. Book introductions and chapter prefaces are offered to provide background material for readers. Chapters are organized around several key questions that are answered with diverse opinions representing all points on the political spectrum. Materials in each chapter include opinions in which authors clearly disagree as well as alternative opinions in which authors may agree on a broader issue but disagree on the possible solutions. In this way, the content of each volume in Current Controversies mirrors the mosaic of opinions encountered in society. Readers will quickly realize that there are many viable answers to these complex issues. By questioning each author's conclusions, students and casual readers can begin to develop the critical thinking skills so important to evaluating opinionated material.

Current Controversies is also ideal for controlled research. Each anthology in the series is composed of primary sources taken from a wide gamut of informational categories including periodicals, newspapers, books, US and foreign government documents, and the publications of private and public organizations. Readers will find factual support for reports, debates, and research papers covering all areas of important issues. In addition, an annotated table of contents, an index, a book and periodical bibliography, and a list of organizations to contact are included in each book to expedite further research.

Perhaps more than ever before in history, people are confronted with diverse and contradictory information. During the Persian Gulf War, for example, the public was not only treated to minute-to-minute coverage of the war, it was also inundated with critiques of the coverage and countless analyses of the factors motivating US involvement. Being able to sort through the plethora of opinions accompanying today's major issues, and to draw one's own conclusions, can be a complicated and frustrating struggle. It is the editors' hope that Current Controversies will help readers with this struggle.

Introduction

> *"Although some would say that the science-fiction concerns about cybercrime have become a reality, not all believe the situation is as dire as often portrayed."*

Prior to the 1980s, there was no word for people who break into a computer system illegally because the computer had yet to become as widespread as it is today. In September 1983, *Newsweek* published an article titled "Beware: Hackers at Play" about the FBI arrest of a group of hackers in Milwaukee accused of (but ultimately not charged with) breaking into several dozen computers. Also in 1983 the movie *WarGames* was released, a science-fiction film about a young hacker who inadvertently breaks into the Pentagon's War Operation Plan Response system. Believing the system to be a game, he causes a nuclear missile scare and nearly starts a world war. In the years since, concerns about cybersecurity have grown, as has the body of legislation to address the issue.

Congress included provisions in the Comprehensive Crime Control Act of 1984 for US Secret Service jurisdiction over computer fraud. Then, in 1986, it passed the Computer Fraud and Abuse Act (CFAA) expanding the scope of protected computers and making it a crime to break into such computer systems. In 1990, Robert Morris Jr. was convicted under CFAA for creating malware that infected more than six hundred thousand computers at US military, academic, and research facilities. He was fined $10,000 and sentenced to three years of probation and community service.

The Computer Security Act of 1987 was passed to improve the security of information in federal computer systems, establishing basic security practices. However, the legislation put the Pentagon only in charge of cybersecurity in matters of national defense, thus leaving the private sector to its own practices.

CFAA has been amended several times. In 1994, the sentences for those who transmit computer viruses were stiffened. Also in that year, the Communications Assistance for Law Enforcement Act required Internet service providers to comply with law enforcement in keeping suspect individuals under surveillance. In 1996, CFAA was amended to allow prosecution of anyone viewing electronic information without authorization, with or without financial gain.

After the 9/11 terrorist attacks, Congress passed the Cyber Security Enhancement Act as part of the Homeland Security Act of 2002. The Cyber Security Enhancement Act gave law enforcement even greater access to personal information through Internet service providers. Also in 2002, Congress passed the Federal Information Security Management Act, which established security requirements for government information technology systems.

Although concern about cybercrime and cybersecurity has grown exponentially since 2002, Congress has not passed any new legislation on the issue. In 2011, the Cyber Intelligence Sharing and Protection Act passed the House of Representatives but was not passed by the Senate. The bill would allow for sharing of Internet traffic information between the US government and private businesses, in an attempt to help ensure the security of networks against cyberattacks. It was reintroduced in 2013 and again passed by the House of Representatives but was not voted on by the Senate. In 2015, the House reintroduced the bill yet again and, as of this writing, it was still in committee. The controversy about the Cyber Intelligence Sharing and Protection Act mirrors the controversy surrounding much of the proposed legislation combating cybercrime: some privacy is sacrificed in the name of security, but not all agree that security should always win.

Although some would say that the science-fiction concerns about cybercrime have become a reality, not all believe the situation is as dire as often portrayed. Many experts agree that cyberattacks are on the rise, but not everyone agrees that this poses a large threat to US security. Similarly, there is debate about the extent to which cybercrime against individuals is a problem. Whether relatively innocuous or not, there are a variety of proposals for protecting national cybersecurity and the security of private Internet users. As the authors of the viewpoints in *Current Controversies: Cybercrime* illustrate, this is a timely debate that changes every day as technology itself changes and society's willingness to accept a certain amount of government intrusion fluctuates.

CHAPTER 1

Does Cybercrime Pose a Serious Problem for US Security?

Cyber Attacks Likely to Increase

Pew Research Center

The Pew Research Center is a nonpartisan fact tank that informs the public about the issues, attitudes, and trends shaping America and the world.

The Internet has become so integral to economic and national life that government, business, and individual users are targets for ever-more frequent and threatening attacks.

In the 10 years since the Pew Research Center and Elon University's Imagining the Internet Center first asked experts about the future of cyber attacks in 2004 a lot has happened:

- Some suspect the Russian government of attacking or encouraging organized crime assaults on official websites in the nation of Georgia during military struggles in 2008 that resulted in a Russian invasion of Georgia.

- In 2009–2010, suspicions arose that a sophisticated government-created computer worm called "Stuxnet" was loosed in order to disable Iranian nuclear plant centrifuges that could be used for making weapons-grade enriched uranium. Unnamed sources and speculators argued that the governments of the United States and Israel might have designed and spread the worm.

- The American Defense Department has created a Cyber Command structure that builds Internet-enabled defensive and offensive cyber strategies as an integral part of war planning and war making.

- In May, five Chinese military officials were indicted in Western Pennsylvania for computer hacking, espionage and other offenses that were aimed at six US victims, including nuclear power plants, metals and solar products industries. The indictment comes after several years of revelations that Chinese military and other agents have broken into computers at major US corporations and media companies in a bid to steal trade secrets and learn what stories journalists were working on.

- In October, Russian hackers were purportedly discovered to be exploiting a flaw in Microsoft Windows to spy on NATO, the Ukrainian government, and Western businesses.

- The respected Ponemon Institute reported in September that 43% of firms in the United States had experienced a data breach in the past year. Retail breaches, in particular, had grown in size in virulence in the previous year. One of the most chilling breaches was discovered in July at JPMorgan Chase & Co., where information from 76 million households and 7 million small businesses was compromised. Obama Administration officials have wondered if the breach was in retaliation by the Putin regime in Russia over events in Ukraine.

- Among the types of exploits of individuals in evidence today are stolen national ID numbers, pilfered passwords and payment information, erased online identities, espionage tools that record all online conversations and keystrokes, and even hacks of driverless cars.

- Days before this report was published, Apple's iCloud cloud-based data storage system was the target of a so-called "man-in-the-middle" attack in China that was aimed at stealing users' passwords and spying on their account activities. Some activists and security experts said they suspected the Chinese government had mounted the attack, perhaps because the iPhone 6 had just become available in the country. Others thought the attack was not sophisticated enough to have been government-initiated.

- The threat of cyber attacks on government agencies, businesses, non-profits, and individual users is so pervasive and worrisome that this month (October 2014) is National Cyber Security Awareness Month.

To explore the future of cyber attacks we canvassed thousands of experts and Internet builders to share their predictions. We call this a canvassing because it is not a representative, randomized survey. Its findings emerge from an "opt in" invitation to experts, many of whom play active roles in Internet evolution as technology builders, researchers, managers, policymakers, marketers, and analysts. We also invited comments from those who have made insightful predictions to our previous queries about the future of the Internet.

There was little disagreement that the spread and importance of the Internet in the lives of people, businesses, and government agencies exposes them all to new dangers.

Overall, 1,642 respondents weighed in on the following question:

Major cyber attacks: By 2025, will a major cyber attack have caused widespread harm to a nation's security and capacity to defend itself and its people? (By "widespread harm," we mean significant loss of life or property losses/damage/theft at the levels of tens of billions of dollars.)

Please elaborate on your answer. (Begin with your name if you are willing to have your comments attributed to you.)

Explain what vulnerabilities nations have to their sovereignty in the coming decade and whether major economic enterprises can or cannot thwart determined opponents. Or explain why you think the level of threat has been hyped and/or why you believe attacks can be successfully thwarted.

Some 61% of these respondents said "yes" that a major attack causing widespread harm would occur by 2025 and 39% said "no."

There was little disagreement that the spread and importance of the Internet in the lives of people, businesses, and government agencies exposes them all to new dangers.

As Jay Cross, the chief scientist at Internet Time Group, summarized his "yes" answer: "Connectedness begets vulnerability."

Or, as Joel Brenner, the former counsel to the National Security Agency explained in the *Washington Post* this past weekend: "The Internet was not built for security, yet we have made it the backbone of virtually all private-sector and government operations, as well as communications. Pervasive connectivity has brought dramatic gains in productivity and pleasure but has created equally dramatic vulnerabilities. Huge heists of personal information are common, and cybertheft of intellectual property and infrastructure penetrations continue at a frightening pace."

There was considerable agreement among the experts in this canvassing that individuals—their accounts and their identities—will be more vulnerable to cyber attacks from bad actors in the future and that businesses will be persistently under attack. Many said the most vulnerable targets include essential utilities. Many also believe that theft at a larger scale than is now being experienced and economic disruptions could be likely.

The experts had varying opinions about the likely extent of damage and disruption possible at the nation-state level. Many argued that cyber attacks between nations have already occurred, often citing as an example the spread of the Stuxnet worm. The respondents also invoked the Cold War as a metaphor as they anticipated the world to come. They argued that the cyber deterrence of mutually assured disruption or destruction would likely keep competing powers from being too aggressive against other nation-states. At the same time, they also anticipate the current cyber arms race dynamic will expand as nations and other groups and individuals ceaselessly work to overcome security measures through the design of potent exploits.

There are serious problems, but it's not clear that those who are directing the hype are focused on the correct problems or solutions.

Some expect that opponents of the political status quo in many regions of the world will work to implement cyber attacks against governments or other entrenched institutions. One "yes" respondent, Dave Kissoondoyal, CEO for KMP Global Ltd., put it this way: "I would not say that a major cyber attack will have caused widespread harm to a nation's security and capacity to defend itself and its people, but the risks will be there. By 2025, there will be widespread use of cyber terrorism and countries will spend a lot of money on cyber security."

Some observed that the Internet's expansion will multiply vulnerabilities of all types, even inside one's home. Tim Kambitsch, an activist Internet user, wrote, "The Internet of Things is just emerging. In the future, control of physical assets, not just information, will be open to cyber attack."

Some respondents who know the technology world well, but are not privy to insider knowledge about cyber threats, expressed uncertainty about the state of things and whether the disaster scenarios that are commonly discussed are hyped or not. The vice president of research and consumer media for a research and analysis firm observed, "There are serious problems, but it's not clear that those who are directing the hype are focused on the correct problems or solutions. So, the problem is both serious and over-hyped."

Security-oriented experts expressed concerns. Jeremy Epstein, a senior computer scientist at SRI International, said, "Damages in the billions will occur to manufacturing and/or utilities but because it ramps up slowly, it will be accepted as just another cost (probably passed on to taxpayers through government rebuilding subsidies and/or environmental damage), and there will be little motivation for the private sector to defend itself. Due to political gridlock and bureaucratic inertia, the government will be unable to defend itself, even if it knows how. The issue is not primarily one of technical capability (although we're sorely lacking in that department). The primary issue is a lack of policy/political/economic incentives and willpower to address the problem."

Cyberwar Is Already Upon Us

John Arquilla

John Arquilla is professor and chair of the Department of Defense Analysis in the Graduate School of Operational and Information Sciences at the Naval Postgraduate School.

In the nearly 20 years since David Ronfeldt and I introduced our concept of cyberwar, this new mode of conflict has become a reality. Cyberwar is here, and it is here to stay, despite what Thomas Rid and other skeptics think.

Back then, we emphasized the growing importance of battlefield information systems and the profound impact their disruption would have in wars large and small. It took just a few years to see how vulnerable the U.S. military had become to this threat. Although most information on cyberwar's repercussions—most notably the 1997 Eligible Receiver exercise—remains classified, suffice it to say that their effect on U.S. forces would be crippling.

Cyberwar waged against one of America's allies has already proved devastating. When Russian tanks rolled into Georgia in 2008, their advance was greatly eased by cyberattacks on Tbilisi's command, control, and communications systems, which were swiftly and nearly completely disrupted. This was the very sort of online assault Ronfeldt and I had envisioned, with blitzkrieg-style operations on the ground augmented by a virtual "bitskrieg."

In some respects, the Russo-Georgian conflict illuminates the potential of cyberwar in a manner not unlike the way the Spanish Civil War foreshadowed the rising dominance of air power 75 years ago, offering a preview of World War II's deadly aerial bombings. Like air warfare, cyberwar will only become more destructive over time. For that reason, the Pentagon was right last year to formally designate cyberspace as a "warfighting domain."

A scaled-up version of this kind of cyberwar, to America-sized attacks, would cause damage in the hundreds of billions of dollars.

These developments align closely with our own predictions two decades ago. But another notion arose alongside ours—that cyberwar is less a way to achieve a winning advantage in battle than a means of covertly attacking the enemy's homeland infrastructure without first having to defeat its land, sea, and air forces in conventional military engagements.

I have been bemused by the high level of attention given to this second mode of "strategic cyberwar." Engaging in disruptive cyberattacks alone is hardly a way to win wars. Think about aerial bombing again: Societies have been standing up to it for the better part of a century, and almost all such campaigns have failed. Civilian populations are just as likely, perhaps even more so, to withstand assaults by bits and bytes. If highly destructive bombing hasn't been able to break the human will, disruptive computer pinging surely won't.

Rid seems especially dubious about the potential for this form of strategic cyberwar. And rightly so. But there is ample evidence that this mode of virtual attack is being employed, and with genuinely damaging effects. The 2007 cyberwar against Estonia, apparently arising out of ethnic Russian anger over removal of a World War II monument, offered a clear example. The attack was initially highly disruptive, forcing the government to take swift, widespread measures to install security patches, improve firewalls, and make strong encryption tools available to the people. Estonia is small, but one of the world's most wired countries; 97 percent of its people do all their banking online. Costs inflicted by the attacks—from business interruption and disruption to the need to erect new defenses—are estimated in the many millions of euros. A scaled-up version of this kind of cyberwar, to America-sized attacks, would cause damage in the hundreds of billions of dollars.

The Stuxnet worm, which struck directly at Iranian nuclear-enrichment capabilities, is another example of strategic cyberattack—what I prefer to call "cybotage." But will it achieve the larger goal of stopping Iranian proliferation efforts? Not on its own, no more than the Israeli air raid on the Osirak nuclear reactor 30 years ago ended the Iraqi nuclear program. Iraq's pursuit of nuclear technology simply became more covert after the Osirak attack, and the same will surely hold true for Iran today.

A key aspect of both Stuxnet and the Estonian cyberattacks is that the identity of the perpetrators, though suspected, cannot be known with certainty. This anonymity is also the case with the extensive cybersnooping campaigns undertaken against sensitive U.S. military systems since the late 1990s—and against leading companies, too, some of which are seeing their intellectual property hemorrhaging out to hackers. A few of these campaigns have suspected links to China and Russia, but nothing is known for sure. So these actions, which to my mind qualify as a low-intensity form of cyberwar, have gone unpunished. Rid himself acknowledges that these sorts of attacks are ongoing, so it seems we are in agreement, at least about the rise of covert cyberwar.

Instead of debating whether [cyberwar] is real, we need to get down to the serious work of better understanding this new mode of war-fighting.

My deeper concern is that these smaller-scale cyberwar exploits might eventually scale up, given the clear vulnerability of advanced militaries and the various communications systems that cover more of the world every day. This is why I think cyberwar is destined to play an increasingly prominent role in future wars. Yes, some cyberweapons do require substantial investment of resources and manpower, as Rid suggests. But once created, they can be used in ways that easily overcome existing defenses. Even for those exploits that don't require significant resources, like the campaign against Estonia, the lesson remains clear: The advantage lies with those who take the offensive.

The challenge for cyberwarriors today lies in figuring out how to thwart these various cyberoffensives. This won't happen if defenders remain dependent on a cyberspace-based version of the Maginot Line: the "firewalls" designed to detect viruses, worms, and other tools, and to keep attackers from intruding into and roaming about one's systems. Like the original Maginot Line, which failed to protect France in World War II, the firewall is easily outflanked. Sadly, undue faith in this passive mode of defense means that, right now, far too much data can be found in fixed places, "at rest." This results in far too much data remaining at risk, easily located and targeted for extraction, manipulation, or destruction. Far better to move away from dependence on firewalls to the ubiquitous use of strong encryption, which protects data with unbreakable codes, and "the cloud," the vast expanse of cyberspace in whose far reaches data can be safely secreted and then swiftly summoned back when needed.

A final aspect of cyberwar that Ronfeldt and I began contemplating so long ago—virtual conflict in the form of society-wide ideological strife—is also coming to pass. Such virtual operations, we wrote back in the early 1990s, would one day extend to "efforts to promote dissident or opposition movements across computer networks." Clearly, we have seen this form of conflict take shape in the "color revolutions" of the past decade and most recently in the Arab Spring; in both cases, the impact of political activism was greatly enhanced by cyber-enabled social networking tools and sites. If there is to be more cyberwar in the future, better it should be what we called "social netwar" than the alternatives.

So, yes, cyberwar has arrived. Instead of debating whether it is real, we need to get down to the serious work of better understanding this new mode of war-fighting, which has been enabled by an information revolution that has brought so much good to the world, but which at the same time heralds an age of perpetual conflict. What we really must ask is: Can cyberwar be controlled? Rid implies that international cooperation to do so is doomed, but I'm not so sure. Pledges not to employ cyberattacks against purely civilian targets, for example, may be genuinely worthwhile—at least for nations, if not for shadowy networks. But networks, too, may come to follow some kind of code of behavior. Even the loosely linked cybervigilante group Anonymous takes considerable pains to explain the rationales for its actions.

So here's hoping that, amid the looming havoc of cyberwars to come, there will also be prospects for cyberpeace.

The Private Sector Is at Risk for Cyberattacks

Daniel J. Gallington

Daniel J. Gallington is the senior policy and program adviser at the George C. Marshall Institute.

Here we go, beating ourselves up over the Edward Snowden-leaked National Security Agency [NSA] programs designed to sort through trillions of telecommunications to find the few related to terrorism. Yet we don't seem at all concerned about how fragile and vulnerable our huge private sector critical cyberinfrastructure, such as our electrical grid, Internet, banking and financial sectors, is to cyberattack.

Not only that, the main reason we haven't been shut down by an external cyberattack by the Russians or the Chinese isn't because they can't do it, but because we are such a fat intelligence target for them. They prefer to be able to steal valuable information from us over the Internet rather than turn it off.

However, assuming things got really ugly, could they shut us down if and when they wanted to? Yes, and it's particularly important that we understand exactly how they could do it and also how we could probably prevent it if we were just a little smarter than we seem to be.

Vulnerability in the Private Sector

First of all, most think that the Defense Department's NSA and Cyber Command are responsible for protecting us from cyberattack. True. However, the "us" part for the NSA is limited to the "dot mil" part of the Internet—at most they protect just the "dot gov" part of our cyberturf.

This leaves the rest of our Internet—i.e., most of it—at a very high degree of risk from cyberattack. Not only that, and surprising as it might be, most of the "dot gov" part doesn't even want the NSA's help in defending its networks, because the NSA typically discovers lots of embarrassing leaks in the communication security of government networks.

Realistically, the odds of the private sector dealing responsibly with these kinds of threats are about as great as General Motors fixing a 57 cent defect in its cars' ignition systems on its own.

The origins of this anomaly go back to when NSA had two basic missions: Collecting signals intelligence, known as "SIGINT," and "communications security," called "COMSEC." In the old days, the second part was very aggressive and put most government telephone users on notice that if they "talked classified" over the unsecured government telephone network, they risked administrative or disciplinary action.

This, as you might imagine, was not at all popular, so over the years the mission was reduced or eliminated throughout the government.

Objecting to my unfavorable characterization of our private sector cyber vulnerabilities, official government spinners will probably say that today we have the Department of Homeland Security, the FBI, the Federal Communications Commission and private contractors working aggressively with the private sector to address and improve the cybersecurity for our private sector infrastructure. However, ask yourself: Do you really believe that, short of a catastrophic shutdown, our private cybersector could be trusted to come forward on its own with, for example, information that security had been compromised, and that, for example, our financial accounts were accessed or our power grid compromised because of an external cyberattack?

What would this do for investor confidence? Realistically, the odds of the private sector dealing responsibly with these kinds of threats are about as great as General Motors fixing a 57 cent defect in its cars' ignition systems on its own. In short, we can't expect them to be honest or objective about it.

A Proactive Approach

So how do we insure our private sector cybernetworks are capable of withstanding or defending themselves against an aggressive external cyberattack like one launched against us because of a rapidly escalating international dispute with China or Russia? Easy. We should be continually testing our critical private infrastructures by simulating external cyberattack. This would be done using the older NSA communications security models as an operational analogy, supplemented with newer and more aggressive oversight and privacy requirements.

As a starter, I have suggested that this be an ongoing joint operation of the FBI, Homeland Security, NSA and the Cyber Command, and be conducted consistent with detailed attorney general privacy guidelines and aggressive oversight by the intelligence, judiciary and homeland security committees of Congress.

In addition, it should be carried out with advance notice to a specific private cybersector or, when centrally managed as part of a carefully coordinated national exercise, our critical private cyberinfrastructure could be "no notice" tested.

This proactive approach may be the only objective way we can be sure our critical private sector cyberinfrastructure can withstand a dedicated external cyberattack and we should be getting busy with it.

This isn't a lesson we need to learn the hard way.

Cyberattacks Could Result in Damage Similar to Natural Disasters

Jeb Boone

Jeb Boone is a correspondent for GlobalPost.

It's a new breed of warfare, unlike anything you've ever seen.

It can threaten a nation's core security, cause mass casualties and weaken the economy, according to the Government Accountability Office, the US Congress' research arm.

Assailants "could gain control of critical switches and derail passenger trains, or trains loaded with lethal chemicals. . . . They could contaminate the water supply in major cities," then-US Defense Secretary Leon Panetta said last October [2012]. Foes could take down electric or water systems, fomenting public panic, reaping high death tolls and causing high physical and economic costs.

It might not even be immediately clear who was behind the attack, or where it was coming from. This devastating power could be wielded with comparatively few operatives, or without the support of a national government. And the massive kinetic strength of the US military would be essentially helpless in thwarting it.

The New Cyber Threats

For more than two decades, internet-based attacks have been relatively infrequent and mostly low level. Now, many experts caution that the specter of cataclysmic cyber war is upon us.

Not everyone agrees with the perilous scenarios; prominent dissenters contend that governments are peddling a trumped-up digital disaster threat to justify privacy intrusions.

One factor that sets cyber assault apart from other forms of warfare is the relative ease in launching it.

But US officials use phrases like "cyber-Pearl Harbor" to describe the threat hackers pose to the critical infrastructure—electricity, water, trains, oil and gas pipelines—and the information networks that run the economy.

World governments have begun taking the threat of cyber war seriously. New specialized military units like the US Cyber Command, South Korea's Cyber Warfare Command and NATO's Computer Incident Response Capability have all begun preparing cyber soldiers.

Responding to the founding of US Cyber Command, China established the now infamous division of the People's Liberation Army dedicated to "defense" against cyber threats.

One factor that sets cyber assault apart from other forms of warfare is the relative ease in launching it. Inducing a catastrophic infrastructure failure may only demand one small change in a line of code.

"We don't even know if you have to have really good network intelligence, be sustainable in your attacks or have persistent access," said Timothy Junio, a research fellow at Stanford University's Center for International Security and Cooperation.

In a nightmare scenario cited by US President Barack Obama, trains carrying hazardous chemicals could derail, contaminating water supplies. Obama last year wrote an op-ed for the *Wall Street Journal* cautioning, "The lack of clean water or functioning hospitals could spark a public health emergency. And as we've seen in past blackouts, the loss of electricity can bring businesses, cities and entire regions to a standstill."

Massive Security Vulnerabilities

Despite the magnitude of the threat, experts contend that the US is woefully under-protected.

They say computer systems that manage critical infrastructure are plagued by security vulnerabilities that would shock anyone with a rudimentary understanding of how to secure a personal computer, let alone a power grid.

A surprising number of systems use passwords hardcoded by the manufacturer—available to hackers via Google search. Other systems use unchanged default username and passwords like "admin/admin."

If passwords aren't publicly available, other glaring vulnerabilities often remain, such as systems "connected to the internet that shouldn't be; people using a workstation that handles physical control at a plant to access their [email]," said Junio.

Users casually browsing the internet on infrastructure workstations need only download a malicious email attachment or click a single malicious link to compromise the security of an entire infrastructural system.

Given that infrastructure systems are remarkably unguarded, the other major hurdle for cyber warriors to surmount is finding the right networks.

"All technical experts agree that critical infrastructure in the US is highly vulnerable," said Junio. "I can't think of any technical study where someone has done penetration testing against a critical infrastructure site and came back saying 'yes this is fine.'"

Part of the reason why systems are so vulnerable is because they were created before widespread use of the internet, and were never designed to be secure in the first place.

"You're taking a system that wasn't meant to be available and now you're making it available, everywhere," said Kevin Albano, a manager of security firm Mandiant's Threat Intelligence division.

Given that infrastructure systems are remarkably unguarded, the other major hurdle for cyber warriors to surmount is finding the right networks.

The Tools Hackers Use

There are plenty of readily available tools that can help.

One of the most effective is called SHODAN. It's available to anyone with web access. SHODAN is used by information security experts to assess whether networks are secure. Consequently, penetration testing tools can be used by hackers in security breaches.

"SHODAN is a search engine for machines connected to the internet. It could be anything from a webcam to a photocopier. It scours the internet looking for IP addresses associated with machines," Junio said. "SHODAN enables hackers to look for targets worldwide, in an automated way, and it's perfectly legal."

Junio noted that during a trip to Taiwan, he discovered that more than 6,000 Taiwanese infrastructure control systems were found in SHODAN—without the government knowing this was a security problem.

In addition to SHODAN, one of the simplest, most common methods used by hackers to gain access to critical infrastructure is a spear phishing attack.

Spear phishing is often successful because it needs to fool only one employee to grant hackers access to an entire system. It works like this: Posing as a colleague, hackers send emails to employees of a utility, asking them to log in to a linked site, using their company username and password. When the unwitting employee logs in, the hacker harvests their password.

Because most people use only one or two passwords for all of their online or company accounts, a single password could give the hacker a way into a system controlling the utility.

Spear phishing attacks are incredibly difficult to defend against because they exploit the likelihood that at least one employee will be fooled.

It doesn't take anything horribly catastrophic to initiate an infrastructure disaster.

Once inside, a small change in a system can potentially cause cascading failures, just as a bird can disrupt electricity for thousands by flying into a transformer.

That's because infrastructure systems "are extremely intertwined," said Robert Bea, risk assessment expert and professor at the University of California at Berkeley. "Should one piece of a system fail, you end up with these cascades, sort of like a game of dominos."

"It doesn't take anything horribly catastrophic to initiate an infrastructure disaster. Using cyber attack methods, individuals with malicious intent could determine the most efficient way to trigger multiple infrastructure failures," Bea added.

What would a cascading failure brought on by a cyber attack look like?

The Potential Damage

According to Bea, it would be very similar to those brought on by natural disasters. To estimate the damage that could be inflicted by a cyber attack triggering a cascading failure, look no further than New Orleans.

"The best reference for me will be Hurricane Katrina and the flood protection system for the Greater New Orleans

Area. . . . Katrina caused a cascade of infrastructure failures that affected the city for months, years. Some are still not working properly," Bea said.

The catastrophic failure of the New Orleans flood levee led to the deaths of more than 1,500 people, in addition to untold billions in economic and environmental damage.

If the catastrophic failure had stemmed from a cyber attack on the systems that controlled the flood levees, the aftermath in New Orleans may have been similar to the failure caused by the hurricane.

While cyber security vulnerabilities in infrastructure systems may only be one problem among many concerning aging infrastructure—the power to unleash another Katrina may rest with hackers, state sponsored or independent, wielding powerful pieces of malware.

That might sound abstract, at least until a major assault occurs. But in 2012, US computers were the target of nearly 9 million malware attacks. And more recently, an attack in South Korea took banks down for days.

Think Again: Cyberwar

Thomas Rid

Thomas Rid is a professor in the Department of War Studies at King's College London.

"Cyberwar Is Already Upon Us."

No way. "Cyberwar is coming!" John Arquilla and David Ronfeldt predicted in a celebrated Rand paper back in 1993. Since then, it seems to have arrived—at least by the account of the U.S. military establishment, which is busy competing over who should get what share of the fight. Cyberspace is "a domain in which the Air Force flies and fights," Air Force Secretary Michael Wynne claimed in 2006. By 2012, William J. Lynn III, the deputy defense secretary at the time, was writing that cyberwar is "just as critical to military operations as land, sea, air, and space." In January, the Defense Department vowed to equip the U.S. armed forces for "conducting a combined arms campaign across all domains—land, air, maritime, space, and cyberspace." Meanwhile, growing piles of books and articles explore the threats of cyberwarfare, cyberterrorism, and how to survive them.

Time for a reality check: Cyberwar is still more hype than hazard. Consider the definition of an act of war: It has to be potentially violent, it has to be purposeful, and it has to be political. The cyberattacks we've seen so far, from Estonia to the Stuxnet virus, simply don't meet these criteria.

Take the dubious story of a Soviet pipeline explosion back in 1982, much cited by cyberwar's true believers as the most destructive cyberattack ever. The account goes like this: In June 1982, a Siberian pipeline that the CIA had virtually

Thomas Rid, "Think Again: Cyberwar," *Foreign Policy*, no. 192, March/April 2012, pp. 80–84. Copyright © 2012 Foreign Policy. All rights reserved. Reproduced with permission.

booby-trapped with a so-called "logic bomb" exploded in a monumental fireball that could be seen from space. The U.S. Air Force estimated the explosion at 3 kilotons, equivalent to a small nuclear device. Targeting a Soviet pipeline linking gas fields in Siberia to European markets, the operation sabotaged the pipeline's control systems with software from a Canadian firm that the CIA had doctored with malicious code. No one died, according to Thomas Reed, a U.S. National Security Council aide at the time who revealed the incident in his 2004 book, *At the Abyss*; the only harm came to the Soviet economy.

There is no known cyberattack that has caused the loss of human life. No cyberoffense has ever injured a person or damaged a building.

But did it really happen? After Reed's account came out, Vasily Pchelintsev, a former KGB head of the Tyumen region, where the alleged explosion supposedly took place, denied the story. There are also no media reports from 1982 that confirm such an explosion, though accidents and pipeline explosions in the Soviet Union were regularly reported in the early 1980s. Something likely did happen, but Reed's book is the only public mention of the incident and his account relied on a single document. Even after the CIA declassified a redacted version of Reed's source, a note on the so-called Farewell Dossier that describes the effort to provide the Soviet Union with defective technology, the agency did not confirm that such an explosion occurred. The available evidence on the Siberian pipeline blast is so thin that it shouldn't be counted as a proven case of a successful cyberattack.

Most other commonly cited cases of cyberwar are even less remarkable. Take the attacks on Estonia in April 2007, which came in response to the controversial relocation of a Soviet war memorial, the *Bronze Soldier*. The well-wired country found itself at the receiving end of a massive distributed denial-of-service attack that emanated from up to 85,000 hijacked computers and lasted three weeks. The attacks reached a peak on May 9, when 58 Estonian websites were attacked at once and the online services of Estonia's largest bank were taken down. "What's the difference between a blockade of harbors or airports of sovereign states and the blockade of government institutions and newspaper websites?" asked Estonian Prime Minister Andrus Ansip.

Despite his analogies, the attack was no act of war. It was certainly a nuisance and an emotional strike on the country, but the bank's actual network was not even penetrated; it went down for 90 minutes one day and two hours the next. The attack was not violent, it wasn't purposefully aimed at changing Estonia's behavior, and no political entity took credit for it. The same is true for the vast majority of cyberattacks on record.

Indeed, there is no known cyberattack that has caused the loss of human life. No cyberoffense has ever injured a person or damaged a building. And if an act is not at least potentially violent, it's not an act of war. Separating war from physical violence makes it a metaphorical notion; it would mean that there is no way to distinguish between World War II, say, and the "wars" on obesity and cancer. Yet those ailments, unlike past examples of cyber "war," actually do kill people.

"A Digital Pearl Harbor Is Only a Matter of Time."

Keep waiting. U.S. Defense Secretary Leon Panetta delivered a stark warning last summer: "We could face a cyberattack that could be the equivalent of Pearl Harbor." Such alarmist predictions have been ricocheting inside the Beltway for the past two decades, and some scaremongers have even upped the ante by raising the alarm about a cyber 9/11. In his 2010 book, *Cyber War*, former White House counterterrorism czar Richard Clarke invokes the specter of nationwide power blackouts, planes falling out of the sky, trains derailing, refineries burning, pipelines exploding, poisonous gas clouds wafting, and satellites spinning out of orbit—events that would make the 2001 attacks pale in comparison.

But the empirical record is less hair-raising, even by the standards of the most drastic example available. Gen. Keith Alexander, head of U.S. Cyber Command (established in 2010 and now boasting a budget of more than $3 billion), shared his worst fears in an April 2011 speech at the University of Rhode Island: "What I'm concerned about are destructive attacks," Alexander said, "those that are coming." He then invoked a remarkable accident at Russia's Sayano-Shushenskaya hydroelectric plant to highlight the kind of damage a cyberattack might be able to cause. Shortly after midnight on Aug. 17, 2009, a 900-ton turbine was ripped out of its seat by a so-called "water hammer," a sudden surge in water pressure that then caused a transformer explosion. The turbine's unusually high vibrations had worn down the bolts that kept its cover in place, and an offline sensor failed to detect the malfunction. Seventy-five people died in the accident, energy prices in Russia rose, and rebuilding the plant is slated to cost $1.3 billion.

Just because there's more malware, however, doesn't mean that attacks are becoming easier.

Tough luck for the Russians, but here's what the head of Cyber Command *didn't* say: The ill-fated turbine had been malfunctioning for some time, and the plant's management was notoriously poor. On top of that, the key event that ultimately triggered the catastrophe seems to have been a fire at Bratsk power station, about 500 miles away. Because the energy supply from Bratsk dropped, authorities remotely increased the burden on the Sayano-Shushenskaya plant. The sudden spike overwhelmed the turbine, which was two months shy of reaching the end of its 30-year life cycle, sparking the catastrophe.

If anything, the Sayano-Shushenskaya incident highlights how difficult a devastating attack would be to mount. The plant's washout was an accident at the end of a complicated and unique chain of events. Anticipating such vulnerabilities in advance is extraordinarily difficult even for insiders; creating comparable coincidences from cyberspace would be a daunting challenge at best for outsiders. If this is the most drastic incident Cyber Command can conjure up, perhaps it's time for everyone to take a deep breath.

"Cyberattacks Are Becoming Easier."

Just the opposite. U.S. Director of National Intelligence James R. Clapper warned last year that the volume of malicious software on American networks had more than tripled since 2009 and that more than 60,000 pieces of malware are now discovered every day. The United States, he said, is undergoing "a phenomenon known as 'convergence,' which amplifies the opportunity for disruptive cyberattacks, including against physical infrastructures." ("Digital convergence" is a snazzy term for a simple thing: more and more devices able to talk to each other, and formerly separate industries and activities able to work together.)

Just because there's more malware, however, doesn't mean that attacks are becoming easier. In fact, potentially damaging or life-threatening cyberattacks should be more difficult to pull off. Why? Sensitive systems generally have built-in redundancy and safety systems, meaning an attacker's likely objective will not be to shut down a system, since merely forcing the shutdown of one control system, say a power plant, could trigger a backup and cause operators to start looking for the bug. To work as an effective weapon, malware would have to influence an active process—but not bring it to a screeching halt. If the malicious activity extends over a lengthy period, it has to remain stealthy. That's a more difficult trick than hitting the virtual off-button.

Take Stuxnet, the worm that sabotaged Iran's nuclear program in 2010. It didn't just crudely shut down the centrifuges at the Natanz nuclear facility; rather, the worm subtly manipulated the system. Stuxnet stealthily infiltrated the plant's networks, then hopped onto the protected control systems, intercepted input values from sensors, recorded these data, and then provided the legitimate controller code with pre-recorded fake input signals, according to researchers who have studied the worm. Its objective was not just to fool operators in a control room, but also to circumvent digital safety and monitoring systems so it could secretly manipulate the actual processes.

As the destructive potential of a cyberweapon grows, the likelihood that it could do far-reaching damage across many systems shrinks.

Building and deploying Stuxnet required extremely detailed intelligence about the systems it was supposed to compromise, and the same will be true for other dangerous cyberweapons. Yes, "convergence," standardization, and sloppy defense of control-systems software *could* increase the risk of generic attacks, but the same trend has also caused defenses against the most coveted targets to improve steadily and has made reprogramming highly specific installations on legacy systems more complex, not less.

"Cyberweapons Can Create Massive Collateral Damage."

Very unlikely. When news of Stuxnet broke, the *New York Times* reported that the most striking aspect of the new weapon was the "collateral damage" it created. The malicious program was "splattered on thousands of computer systems around the world, and much of its impact has been on those systems, rather than on what appears to have been its intended target, Iranian equipment," the *Times* reported. Such descriptions encouraged the view that computer viruses are akin to highly contagious biological viruses that, once unleashed from the lab, will turn against all vulnerable systems, not just their intended targets.

But this metaphor is deeply flawed. As the destructive potential of a cyberweapon grows, the likelihood that it could do far-reaching damage across many systems shrinks. Stuxnet did infect more than 100,000 computers—mainly in Iran, Indonesia, and India, though also in Europe and the United States. But it was so specifically programmed that it didn't actually damage those machines, afflicting only Iran's centrifuges at Natanz. The worm's aggressive infection strategy was designed to maximize the likelihood that it would reach its intended target. Because that final target was not networked, "all the functionality required to sabotage a system was embedded directly in the Stuxnet executable," the security software company Symantec observed in its analysis of the worm's code. So yes, Stuxnet was "splattered" far and wide, but it only executed its damaging payload where it was supposed to.

Collateral infection, in short, is not necessarily collateral damage. A sophisticated piece of malware may aggressively infect many systems, but if there is an intended target, the infection will likely have a distinct payload that will be harmless to most computers. Especially in the context of more sophisticated cyberweapons, the image of inadvertent collateral damage doesn't hold up. They're more like a flu virus that only makes one family sick.

"In Cyberspace, Offense Dominates Defense."

Wrong again. The information age has "offense-dominant attributes," Arquilla and Ronfeldt wrote in their influential 1996 book, *The Advent of Netwar*. This view has spread through the

American defense establishment like, well, a virus. A 2011 Pentagon report on cyberspace stressed "the advantage currently enjoyed by the offense in cyberwarfare." The intelligence community stressed the same point in its annual threat report to Congress last year, arguing that offensive tactics—known as vulnerability discovery and exploitation—are evolving more rapidly than the federal government and industry can adapt their defensive best practices. The conclusion seemed obvious: Cyberattackers have the advantage over cyberdefenders, "with the trend likely getting worse over the next five years."

Even if it were possible to distinguish criminal from state-sponsored political activity, they often use the same means.

A closer examination of the record, however, reveals three factors that put the offense at a disadvantage. First is the high cost of developing a cyberweapon, in terms of time, talent, and target intelligence needed. Stuxnet, experts speculate, took a superb team and a lot of time. Second, the potential for generic offensive weapons may be far smaller than assumed for the same reasons, and significant investments in highly specific attack programs may be deployable only against a very limited target set. Third, once developed, an offensive tool is likely to have a far shorter half-life than the defensive measures put in place against it. Even worse, a weapon may only be able to strike a single time; once the exploits of a specialized piece of malware are discovered, the most critical systems will likely be patched and fixed quickly. And a weapon, even a potent one, is not much of a weapon if an attack cannot be repeated. Any political threat relies on the credible threat to attack or to replicate a successful attack. If that were in doubt, the coercive power of a cyberattack would be drastically reduced.

"We Need a Cyberarms Control Agreement."

We don't. Cyberwar alarmists want the United States to see cybersecurity as a new challenge on a geopolitical scale. They see cyberspace becoming a new area for military competition with rivals such as Russia and China, and they believe new cyber-arms limitation agreements are needed to prevent this. There are some rumblings to establish international norms on this topic: The British government convened a conference in London in late 2011, originally intended to make the Internet more secure by agreeing on new rules of the road, and Russia and China proposed at the U.N. General Assembly last September the establishment of an "international code of conduct for information security." Now, diplomats are debating whether the United Nations should try to forge the equivalent of nuclear arms control in cyberspace.

So, should it? The answer is no. Attempts to limit cyber-weapons through international agreements have three principal problems. The first difficulty is drawing the line between cybercrime and potentially political activity in cyberspace. In January, for instance, a Saudi hacker stole about 20,000 Israeli credit card numbers from a shopping website and leaked the information to the public. In retaliation, a group of Israeli hackers broke into Saudi shopping sites and threatened to release private credit card information.

Where is the dividing line? Even if it were possible to distinguish criminal from state-sponsored political activity, they often use the same means. A second hitch is practical: Verification would be impossible. Accurately counting the size of nuclear arsenals and monitoring enrichment activities is already a huge challenge; installing cameras to film programmers and "verify" they don't design malicious software is a pipe dream.

The third problem is political, and even more fundamental: Cyberaggressors may act politically, but in sharp contrast with warfare, they are likely to have a strong interest in *avoiding* attribution. Subversion has always thrived in cyberspace because preserving one's anonymity is easier to achieve than ironclad attribution. That's the root of the political problem: Having a few states agree on cyberarms limitation is about as realistic as a treaty to outlaw espionage and about as practical as outlawing the general subversion of established order.

Cybersecurity has a broader meaning in non-democracies: For them, the worst-case scenario is not collapsing power plants, but collapsing political power.

"The West Is Falling Behind Russia and China."

Yes, but not how you think. Russia and China are busy sharpening their cyberweapons and are already well steeped in using them. The Russian military clandestinely crippled Estonia's economy in 2007 and Georgia's government and banks in 2008. The People's Liberation Army's numerous Chinese cyberwarriors have long inserted "logic bombs" and "trapdoors" into America's critical infrastructure, lying dormant and ready to wreak havoc on the country's grid and bourse in case of a crisis. Both countries have access to technology, cash, and talent—and have more room for malicious maneuvers than lawabiding Western democracies poised to fight cyberwar with one hand tied behind their backs.

Or so the alarmists tell us. Reality looks quite different. Stuxnet, by far the most sophisticated cyberattack on record, was most likely a U.S.-Israeli operation. Yes, Russia and China have demonstrated significant skills in cyberespionage, but the fierceness of Eastern cyberwarriors and their coded weaponry is almost certainly overrated. When it comes to military-grade offensive attacks, America and Israel seem to be well ahead of the curve.

Ironically, it's a different kind of cybersecurity that Russia and China may be more worried about. Why is it that those countries, along with such beacons of liberal democracy as Uzbekistan, have suggested that the United Nations establish an "international code of conduct" for cybersecurity? Cyberespionage was elegantly ignored in the suggested wording for the convention, as virtual break-ins at the Pentagon and Google remain a favorite official and corporate pastime of both countries. But what Western democracies see as constitutionally protected free speech in cyberspace, Moscow and Beijing regard as a new threat to their ability to control their citizens. Cybersecurity has a broader meaning in non-democracies: For them, the worst-case scenario is not collapsing power plants, but collapsing political power.

The social media-fueled Arab Spring has provided dictators with a case study in the need to patrol cyberspace not only for subversive code, but also for subversive ideas. The fall of Egypt's Hosni Mubarak and Libya's Muammar al-Qaddafi surely sent shivers down the spines of officials in Russia and China. No wonder the two countries asked for a code of conduct that helps combat activities that use communications technologies—"including networks" (read: social networks)—to undermine "political, economic and social stability."

So Russia and China are ahead of the United States, but mostly in defining cybersecurity as the fight against subversive behavior. This is the true cyberwar they are fighting.

The Risk of Cyberattacks Is Exaggerated

Martin C. Libicki

Martin C. Libicki is a professor at the Frederick S. Pardee RAND Graduate School in Santa Monica, California.

These days, most of Washington seems to believe that a major cyberattack on U.S. critical infrastructure is inevitable. In March [2013], James Clapper, U.S. director of national intelligence, ranked cyberattacks as the greatest short-term threat to U.S. national security. General Keith Alexander, the head of the U.S. Cyber Command, recently characterized "cyber exploitation" of U.S. corporate computer systems as the "greatest transfer of wealth in world history." And in January [2013], a report by the Pentagon's Defense Science Board argued that cyber risks should be managed with improved defenses and deterrence, including "a nuclear response in the most extreme case."

The Perception of Risk

Although the risk of a debilitating cyberattack is real, the perception of that risk is far greater than it actually is. No person has ever died from a cyberattack, and only one alleged cyberattack has ever crippled a piece of critical infrastructure, causing a series of local power outages in Brazil. In fact, a major cyberattack of the kind intelligence officials fear has not taken place in the 21 years since the Internet became accessible to the public.

Thus, while a cyberattack could theoretically disable infrastructure or endanger civilian lives, its effects would unlikely reach the scale U.S. officials have warned of. The immediate and direct damage from a major cyberattack on the United States could range anywhere from zero to tens of billions of dollars, but the latter would require a broad outage of electric power or something of comparable damage. Direct casualties would most likely be limited, and indirect causalities would depend on a variety of factors such as whether the attack disabled emergency 911 dispatch services. Even in that case, there would have to be no alternative means of reaching first responders for such an attack to cause casualties. The indirect effects might be greater if a cyberattack caused a large loss of confidence, particularly in the banking system. Yet scrambled records would probably prove insufficient to incite a run on the banks.

Among the world's potential interstate confrontations, one between the United States and Iran has the greatest potential for a significant cyber component.

Officials also warn that the United States might not be able to identify the source of a cyberattack as it happens or in its immediate aftermath. Cyberattacks have neither fingerprints nor the smell of gunpowder, and hackers can make an intrusion appear legitimate or as if it came from somewhere else. Iran, for example, may not have known why its centrifuges were breaking down prematurely before its officials read about the covert cyber-sabotage campaign against the country's nuclear program in *The New York Times*. Victims of advanced persistent threats—extended intrusions into organization networks for the purpose of espionage—are often unaware for months, or even years, that their servers have been penetrated. The reason that such attacks go undetected is because the removal of information does not affect the information in the system, so nothing seems amiss. The exfiltration of information can also be easily hidden, such as in the daily flow of web traffic from an organization.

But since everything is becoming increasingly dependent on computers, could levels of damage impossible today become inevitable tomorrow? As it happens, all of the trend lines—good and bad—in cyberspace are rising simultaneously: the sophistication of attackers, but also that of the defenders; the salience of cyberattacks as weapons, but also the awareness of the threat they pose; the bandwidth available for organizing larger attacks, but also the resources to ward them off. It is bad news that Iran is beginning to see cyberwar as a deniable means of exploiting easy targets. And it is good news that software companies are now rethinking the architectural features of their systems that permit such vulnerabilities to exist in the first place.

A Confrontation with Iran

Among the world's potential interstate confrontations, one between the United States and Iran has the greatest potential for a significant cyber component. Indeed, Iran has already started to flex its muscles in cyberspace. In late 2012, cyberattackers linked to Iran penetrated the network of Aramco, Saudi Arabia's national oil and gas company, effectively trashing 30,000 computers. Rasgas, a Qatari corporation, faced similar treatment. This spring, anonymous U.S. officials claimed that Iranian hackers were able to gain access to control-system software that could allow them to manipulate U.S. oil and gas pipelines.

And Iran has plenty of reasons to launch a cyberattack against the United States. For one, Tehran has not forgotten Stuxnet, a U.S. cyberattack on Iran's uranium enrichment facility at Natanz in 2009. Through a cyberattack on the U.S. homeland, Iran could exact revenge and signal to those who would consider attacking its nuclear program—whether by airstrike or cyberattack—that they cannot move against Iran with impunity. Iran might also seek to undermine U.S. preparations for a preventive strike on its nuclear program. In this case, Iran could also hope to distract political leaders in Washington; give U.S. allies second thoughts about supporting U.S. military action; and divert a potential strike against Iranian nuclear sites, reasoning that the United States would respond by counterattacking Iran's cyberinfrastructure instead.

The United States can best mitigate the risks of cyberwar by adopting technical and political measures to discourage cyberattacks before they happen.

It is here that the greatest risk of a cyberconflict comes in, one that has less to do with the initial damage than with how the United States would choose to respond. Determining that a cyberattack is an act of war would be more than just a conclusion; it is a decision that could initiate a war of choice. Even if an attack occurred during a burgeoning U.S.-Iran crisis, the United States might still not be able to attribute the attack directly to the Iranian government; other states, non-state actors, or rogue elements within Iran may have their own reasons for lighting matches. Retaliation would therefore be risky.

In addition, a retaliatory cyberattack could quickly push both sides up the escalation ladder and even draw in third parties. If the Iranians considered cyberattacks to be a form of terrorism, they could respond by ramping up their sponsorship of conventional terrorist attacks. The United States, too, might decide to abandon virtual war for real war, as current U.S. policy allows for conventional military responses to cyberattacks. That would further poison U.S.-Iranian relations to such an extent that the next crisis in the physical world could be increasingly difficult to manage. Bluntly put, it might not be worth risking all these consequences in order to reduce the odds that Iran could, from time to time, attack U.S. computers.

Preventing the Probable

The United States can best mitigate the risks of cyberwar by adopting technical and political measures to discourage cyberattacks before they happen.

The U.S. government could invest resources to reduce vulnerabilities in commercial software, encourage better management of cyber systems, and develop security tools that can quickly detect and thwart attacks in progress.

Stronger regulations and incentives in the private sector would also be crucial: Nearly all of the critical systems in the United States remain in private hands, and nearly all critical software is developed privately. Sharing intelligence with potential victims would also be useful, but not nearly as much as sharing information on vulnerabilities with those who write and maintain the software that can be exploited in an attack.

Technical capabilities can also create political deterrents. If the United States is able to better identify the sources of cyberattacks, it can give a clearer impression that it might retaliate, giving its enemies more inhibitions about attacking in the first place. Rhetoric also has a role to play in keeping potential attackers at bay. Washington should make a clear distinction between cyber-espionage (which it has not retaliated against) and cyberattacks, since doing so would leave open the possibility that the latter crosses a red line and could be matched with a disproportionately harsh response.

At the same time, the United States should leave room for operational flexibility. Leaders should avoid acting too hastily out of fear that hesitation will lead to disaster—and, if anything, fear the opposite. Washington need not take possession of a crisis unnecessarily; otherwise, it risks backing itself into a corner where it has no choice but to respond, regardless of whether doing so is wise. In some cases, a well-crafted narrative—for example, one that emphasizes the role of inadvertence or rogue actors—might allow the attacker to cease attacks without losing face. Escalation, although necessary in some cases, can carry many unintended consequences.

Computers may work in nanoseconds, but the true target of any response is not cyberweapons—it is the people who wield them. Even if a computer is destroyed, a substitute may be close at hand. Human beings, unlike computers, do not work in nanoseconds. Persuasion and dissuasion in cyberwar take as much time as in wars of any other form.

CHAPTER 2

Is Cybercrime Against Individuals a Serious Problem?

Overview: Hacking Tops List of Crimes Americans Worry About Most

Rebecca Riffkin

Rebecca Riffkin is a journalist and analyst at Gallup.

As the list of major U.S. retailers hit by credit card hackers continues to grow this year, Americans are more likely to worry about having credit card information they used in stores stolen by computer hackers than any other crime they are asked about. Sixty-nine percent of Americans report they frequently or occasionally worry about this happening to them. Having a computer or smartphone hacked (62%) is the only other crime that worries the majority of Americans.

Less than half of Americans worry at least occasionally about other crimes, ranging from 45% who worry about their home being burglarized when they are not there to 7% who worry about being assaulted by a coworker on the job.

Gallup updated its measure of Americans' worry about a number of crime scenarios in its annual Crime poll, conducted Oct. 12–15. Trends on Americans' worries about most of these crimes extend back to 2000, although this was the first year Gallup asked Americans about having credit card information stolen or a smartphone or computer hacked.

Upper-income Americans, those whose household incomes are $75,000 or more a year, are more likely than lower-income Americans to worry frequently or occasionally about hacking of their credit card information, 85% to 50%. Americans between the ages of 30 and 64 worry about this more than younger and older Americans do.

Higher levels of worry about credit card and computer-related crimes among upper-income Americans may result from their higher daily spending. Additionally, lower-income Americans are less likely to own credit cards or smartphones. In April, 58% of Americans whose annual household incomes are less than $30,000 said they owned no credit cards, compared with 11% of upper-income Americans. In December 2013, Gallup found that upper-income Americans are also more likely than lower-income Americans to own a smartphone, 84% vs. 46%.

The Department of Homeland Security estimates that more than 1,000 U.S. businesses have been hit by cyber-attacks similar to the one that hit U.S. retailer Target.

More than One in Four Americans Say They Have Been Hacked

Americans may be more worried about hacking because a relatively high percentage of them say they have had their information hacked. A quarter of Americans, 27%, say they or another household member had information from a credit card used at a store stolen by computer hackers during the last year—making this the most frequently experienced crime on a list of nine crimes. Eleven percent say they or a household member have had their computer or smartphone hacked in the last year, also in the top half of crimes on the list.

Although a relatively high percentage of Americans say they have been hacking victims, relatively low percentages say they reported it to the police. Slightly less than half of Americans (45%) who say they had credit card information stolen say they reported it to the police. And about a quarter of victims say they notified police about their computer or smartphone being hacked. Of Americans who say they were victims of other crimes in the last year, including stolen cars, muggings, or burglaries, an average of two-thirds say they reported them to police, higher than what Gallup finds for hacking crimes.

One reason reporting of credit card information theft may be lower is that some Americans who are victims of these crimes may not have seen monetary losses. The Department of Homeland Security estimates that more than 1,000 U.S. businesses have been hit by cyberattacks similar to the one that hit U.S. retailer Target; the Target breach alone is estimated to have affected 40 million credit and debit card accounts. Although this is a large proportion of Americans whose information could have been affected, it is unknown how many actually saw these cards used for fraudulent purchases.

Bottom Line

Americans today are more worried about their credit card information being hacked from stores than about any other crimes they are asked about, and a relatively high percentage say they have been victims of this hacking. Many high-profile and popular stores and restaurants have had major hacking problems in 2013 and 2014, something that no doubt has helped kindle such fears.

With credit card hacking clearly a concern to many Americans, it may affect their shopping habits as they take measures to protect their identities and finances. Consumers may avoid stores that have been hacked, and begin paying more frequently with cash or prepaid cards to protect their identities. To protect their customers and themselves, some credit card companies are switching to security chips, which are more secure than the magnetic strips currently common in the U.S., and are cautioning customers to check their accounts for suspicious activity.

Cyberattacks to Steal Customer Information Are a Serious Problem

Riley Walters

Riley Walters is a research assistant at the Douglas and Sarah Allison Center for Foreign and National Security Policy at The Heritage Foundation.

The spate of recent data breaches at big-name companies such as JPMorgan Chase, Home Depot, and Target raises questions about the effectiveness of the private sector's information security. According to FBI Director James Comey, "There are two kinds of big companies in the United States. There are those who've been hacked ... and those who don't know they've been hacked."

A recent survey by the Ponemon Institute showed the average cost of cyber crime for U.S. retail stores more than doubled from 2013 to an annual average of $8.6 million per company in 2014. The annual average cost per company of successful cyber attacks increased to $20.8 million in financial services, $14.5 million in the technology sector, and $12.7 million in communications industries.

Cyber Attacks in 2014

This paper lists known cyber attacks on private U.S. companies since the beginning of 2014. (A companion paper discussed cyber breaches in the federal government.) By its very nature, a list of this sort is incomplete. The scope of many attacks is not fully known. For example, in July [2014], the U.S. Computer Emergency Readiness Team issued an advisory that

Riley Walters, "Cyber Attacks on US Companies in 2014," heritage.org, *Issue Brief*, no. 4289, October 27, 2014, pp. 1–5. Copyright © 2014 The Heritage Foundation. All rights reserved. Reproduced with permission.

more than 1,000 U.S. businesses have been affected by the Backoff malware, which targets point-of-sale (POS) systems used by most retail industries. These attacks targeted administrative and customer data and, in some cases, financial data.

Between July and October 2013, the credit card information of 350,000 [Neiman Marcus customers] was stolen, and more than 9,000 of the credit cards have been used fraudulently since the attack.

This list includes only cyber attacks that have been made known to the public. Most companies encounter multiple cyber attacks every day, many unknown to the public and many unknown to the companies themselves.

The data breaches below are listed chronologically by month of public notice.

January

- *Target (retail).* In January, Target announced an additional 70 million individuals' contact information was taken during the December 2013 breach, in which 40 million customer's credit and debit card information was stolen.

- *Neiman Marcus (retail).* Between July and October 2013, the credit card information of 350,000 individuals was stolen, and more than 9,000 of the credit cards have been used fraudulently since the attack. Sophisticated code written by the hackers allowed them to move through company computers, undetected by company employees for months.

- *Michaels (retail).* Between May 2013 and January 2014, the payment cards of 2.6 million Michaels customers were affected. Attackers targeted the Michaels POS system to gain access to their systems.

- *Yahoo! Mail (communications)*. The e-mail service for 273 million users was reportedly hacked in January, although the specific number of accounts affected was not released.

April

- *Aaron Brothers (retail)*. The credit and debit card information for roughly 400,000 customers of Aaron Brothers, a subsidiary of Michaels, was compromised by the same POS system malware.

- *AT&T (communications)*. For two weeks AT&T was hacked from the inside by personnel who accessed user information, including social security information.

May

- *eBay (retail)*. Cyber attacks in late February and early March led to the compromise of eBay employee log-ins, allowing access to the contact and log-in information for 233 million eBay customers. eBay issued a statement asking all users to change their passwords.

- *Five Chinese hackers indicted*. Five Chinese nationals were indicted for computer hacking and economic espionage of U.S. companies between 2006 and 2014. The targeted companies included Westinghouse Electric (energy and utilities), U.S. subsidiaries of SolarWorld AG (industrial), United States Steel (industrial), Allegheny Technologies (technology), United Steel Workers Union (services), and Alcoa (industrial).

- *Unnamed public works (energy and utilities)*. According to the Department of Homeland Security, an unnamed public utility's control systems were accessed by hackers through a brute-force attack on employee's log-in passwords.

June

- *Feedly (communications).* Feedly's 15 million users were temporarily affected by three distributed denial-of-service attacks.

- *Evernote (technology).* In the same week as the Feedly cyber attack, Evernote and its 100 million users faced a similar denial-of-service attack.

- *P.F. Chang's China Bistro (restaurant).* Between September 2013 and June 2014, credit and debit card information from 33 P.F. Chang's restaurants was compromised and reportedly sold online.

August

- *U.S. Investigations Services (services).* U.S. Investigations Services, a subcontractor for federal employee background checks, suffered a data breach in August, which led to the theft of employee personnel information. Although no specific origin of attack was reported, the company believes the attack was state-sponsored.

- *Community Health Services (health care).* At Community Health Service (CHS), the personal data for 4.5 million patients were compromised between April and June. CHS warns that any patient who visited any of its 206 hospital locations over the past five years may have had his or her data compromised. The sophisticated malware used in the attack reportedly originated in China. The FBI warns that other health care firms may also have been attacked.

- *UPS (services).* Between January and August, customer information from more than 60 UPS stores was compromised, including financial data, reportedly as a result of the Backoff malware attacks.

- *Defense Industries (defense).* Su Bin, a 49-year-old Chinese national, was indicted for hacking defense companies such as Boeing. Between 2009 and 2013, Bin reportedly worked with two other hackers in an attempt to steal manufacturing plans for defense programs, such as the F-35 and F-22 fighter jets.

September

- *Home Depot (retail).* Cyber criminals reportedly used malware to compromise the credit card information for roughly 56 million shoppers in Home Depot's 2,000 U.S. and Canadian outlets.

- *Google (communications).* Reportedly, 5 million Gmail usernames and passwords were compromised. About 100,000 were released on a Russian forum site.

- *Apple iCloud (technology).* Hackers reportedly used passwords hacked with brute-force tactics and third-party applications to access Apple user's online data storage, leading to the subsequent posting of celebrities' private photos online. It is uncertain whether users or Apple were at fault for the attack.

- *Goodwill Industries International (retail).* Between February 2013 and August 2014, information for roughly 868,000 credit and debit cards was reportedly stolen from 330 Goodwill stores. Malware infected the chain store through infected third-party vendors.

- *SuperValu (retail).* SuperValu was attacked between June and July, and suffered another malware attack between late August and September. The first theft included customer and payment card information from some of its Cub Foods, Farm Fresh, Shop 'n Save, and Shoppers stores. The second attack reportedly involved only payment card data.

- *Bartell Hotels (hotel).* The information for up to 55,000 customers was reportedly stolen between February and May.

- *U.S. Transportation Command contractors (transportation).* A Senate report revealed that networks of the U.S. Transportation Command's contractors were successfully breached 50 times between June 2012 and May 2013. At least 20 of the breaches were attributed to attacks originating from China.

October

- *J.P. Morgan Chase (financial).* An attack in June was not noticed until August. The contact information for 76 million households and 7 million small businesses was compromised. The hackers may have originated in Russia and may have ties to the Russian government.

- *Dairy Queen International (restaurant).* Credit and debit card information from 395 Dairy Queen and Orange Julius stores was compromised by the Backoff malware.

- *Snapsave (communications).* Reportedly, the photos of 200,000 users were hacked from Snapsave, a third-party app for saving photos from Snapchat, an instant photo-sharing app.

Securing Information

As cyber attacks on retail, technology, and industrial companies increase so does the importance of cybersecurity. From brute-force attacks on networks to malware compromising credit card information to disgruntled employees sabotaging their companies' networks from the inside, companies and their customers need to secure their data. To improve the private sector's ability to defend itself, Congress should:

- *Create a safe legal environment for sharing information.* As the leaders of technological growth, private companies are in most ways at the forefront of cyber security. Much like government agencies, companies must share information that concerns cyber threats and attack among themselves and with appropriate private-public organizations. Congress needs to create a safe environment in which companies can voluntarily share information without fear of legal or regulatory backlash.

- *Work with international partners.* As with the Backoff malware attacks, attacks can affect hundreds if not thousands of individual networks. These infected networks can then infect companies outside the U.S. and vice versa. U.S. and foreign companies and governments need to work together to increase overall cybersecurity and to enable action against individual cyber criminals and known state-sponsored cyber aggressors.

- *Encourage cyber insurance.* Successful cyber attacks are inevitable because no security is perfect. With the number of breaches growing daily, a cybersecurity insurance market is developing to mitigate the cost of breaches. Congress and the Administration should encourage the proper allocation of liability and the establishment of a cyber insurance system to mitigate faulty cyber practices and human error.

The recent increases in the rate and the severity of cyber attacks on U.S. companies indicate a clear threat to businesses and customers. As businesses come to terms with the increasing threat of hackers, instituting the right policies is critical to harnessing the power of the private sector. In a cyber environment with ever-changing risks and threats, the government needs to do more to support the private sector in establishing sound cybersecurity while not creating regulations that hinder businesses more than help them.

Online Sexual Predators Are a Serious Problem

Federal Bureau of Investigation

The Federal Bureau of Investigation (FBI) is the domestic intelligence and security service of the United States, which serves as the main federal law enforcement agency.

It's a recipe for trouble: naive teenagers, predatory adults, and a medium—the Internet—that easily connects them.

Pedophiles Are Online

"It's an unfortunate fact of life that pedophiles are everywhere online," said Special Agent Greg Wing, who supervises a cyber squad in our Chicago Field Office.

When a young person visits an online forum for a popular teen singer or actor, Wing said, "Parents can be reasonably certain that online predators will be there." It is believed that more than half a million pedophiles are online every day.

Agents assigned to our Innocent Images National Initiative are working hard to catch these child predators and to alert teens and parents about the dark side of the Internet—particularly when it comes to social networking sites and, increasingly, online gaming forums.

Pedophiles go where children are. Before the Internet, that meant places such as amusement parks and zoos. Today, the virtual world makes it alarmingly simple for pedophiles—often pretending to be teens themselves—to make contact with young people.

Even without being someone's "friend" online, which allows access to one's social networking space, pedophiles can see a trove of teenagers' personal information—the town they

Federal Bureau of Investigation, "Child Predators: The Online Threat Continues to Grow," May 17, 2011.

live in, the high school they attend, their favorite music and TV programs—because the youngsters often post it for anyone to see.

There are basically two types of pedophiles on the Internet—those who seek face-to-face meetings with children and those who are content to anonymously collect and trade child pornography images.

"The younger generation wants to express themselves, and they don't realize how vulnerable it makes them," Wing said.

Two Types of Pedophiles

For a pedophile, that personal information is like gold and can be used to establish a connection and gain a child's trust.

There are basically two types of pedophiles on the Internet—those who seek face-to-face meetings with children and those who are content to anonymously collect and trade child pornography images.

Those seeking face-to-face meetings create bogus identities online, sometimes posing as teenagers. Then they troll the Internet for easy victims—youngsters with low self-esteem, problems with their parents, or a shortage of money. The pedophile might find a 14-year-old girl, for example, who has posted seemingly harmless information on her space for anyone to see. The pedophile sends a message saying he goes to high school in a nearby town and likes the same music or TV shows she likes.

Then the pedophile cultivates a friendly online relationship that investigators call "grooming." It could continue for days or weeks before the pedophile begins bringing up sexual topics, asking for explicit pictures or for a personal meeting. By that time an emotional connection has been made—and pedophiles can be master manipulators. Even if an actual meeting never takes place, it is important to note that youngsters can be victimized by such sexually explicit online contact.

The Need for Vigilance

Even worse than posting personal information for anyone to see is the fact that many youngsters will accept "friends" who are total strangers. "Nobody wants to just have five friends online," Wing said. "It's a popularity thing."

Special Agent Wesley Tagtmeyer, a veteran cyber investigator in our Chicago office who works undercover during online investigations, said that in his experience, about 70 percent of youngsters will accept "friend" requests regardless of whether they know the requester.

Tagtmeyer and other cyber investigators say a relatively new trend among pedophiles is to begin grooming youngsters through online gaming forums, some of which allow two-way voice and video communication. Parents who might be vigilant about monitoring their children's Internet activity often have no idea that online video gaming platforms can pose a threat.

"Parents need to talk to their children about these issues," he said. "It's no longer enough to keep computers in an open area of the house so they can be monitored. The same thing needs to be done with online gaming platforms."

Concerns About Cyberattacks Are Often Driven by Misinformation

P.W. Singer

P.W. Singer is director of the Center for 21st Century Security and Intelligence at the Brookings Institution and coauthor of the book Cybersecurity and Cyberwar: What Everyone Needs to Know.

A recent Pew poll found that Americans are more afraid of a cyber attack than they are of Iranian nuclear weapons, the rise of China or climate change. Such fears are not only out of proportion to risk; if they take hold, they could threaten the positive gains of the digital age.

A Lack of Knowledge

Certainly there are growing threats in the cyber world, and the stakes are high. But there is also a high level of misinformation and plain old ignorance driving the fear. Despite the Internet now enabling us to run down the answers to almost any question, a number of myths have emerged about online security and what it means for us offline. The result is that some threats are overblown and overreacted to, while other quite legitimate ones are ignored.

Every computer user has had to make cyber-security decisions: whether to trust online vendors with credit card information and how often to change an email password, to name two. But these decisions are too often based on scant understanding.

The problem is even more acute in business and government. Some 70% of executives have made a cyber-security decision of some sort for their firms. Yet MBA [Master of Business Administration] programs still aren't routinely teaching cyber security as part of normal management responsibility, nor do the schools that train diplomats, lawyers, generals, journalists and others who have to make important decisions in this regard every day. Whether in the boardroom or the White House situation room, crucial matters are often handed off to so-called experts, which is a good way to be taken advantage of—and to feel more secure than you actually are.

Despite its central position in both congressional testimony and Hollywood movies, no person has actually been hurt or killed by an act of cyber terrorism.

Instead of focusing on what we need to learn, we've instead fed on hype that fuels fears but doesn't solve problems. For instance, Americans have repeatedly been told by government leaders and media pundits that cyber attacks are like weapons of mass destruction and that we are in a sort of Cold War of cyberspace.

But the zeros and ones of malware are nothing like the physics of nuclear weapons, nor are the political dynamics they fuel. Moreover, the globalized network in which the NSA [National Security Agency], Chinese hackers, Anonymous, Google, Target and you and I all play is hardly the kind of bipolar world that spawned the Cold War.

There is certainly a battle of ideas online, but it's as likely to focus on which boy Katniss of *The Hunger Games* should choose in the end (Peeta, of course) as it is to focus on competing political visions. Rather than looking to the Dr. Strangelove era of the Cold War for inspiration, we'd be better off studying other historical lessons, focusing on how the government has effectively approached other new problem areas, from how the seas were made safe to the success story of the Centers for Disease Control and Prevention in public health.

The Need for Resilience

Despite its central position in both congressional testimony and Hollywood movies, no person has actually been hurt or killed by an act of cyber terrorism. Indeed, squirrels have taken down power grids, but hackers never have. But that is not to say there's no threat. Indeed, our own creation, the Stuxnet worm, which attacked Iran's nuclear infrastructure, demonstrated that cyber weapons can cause damage.

But the fiction of a "cyber Pearl Harbor" gets far more attention than the real, and arguably far greater, impact of the massive campaign of intellectual property theft emanating from China. As with 9/11, the way that we react (or overreact) to an attack, terrorist or otherwise, is what truly determines the impact of it. Understanding the difference between hackers doing something annoying and doing something with the capacity to cause serious harm will better direct our fears and resources.

Cyber security has to be seen as a management problem that will never go away. As long as we use the Internet, there will be cyber risks. The key is to move away from a mentality of seeking silver bullets and ever-higher walls and instead to focus on the most important feature of true cyber security: resilience. In both the real and online worlds, we can't stop or deter all bad things, but we can plan for and deal with them.

In treating cyber security as a matter only for IT experts, computer users often neglect the most basic precautions that go a long way toward protecting both the Internet's users and the network itself. Indeed, one study found that as much as 94% of attacks could be stopped with basic "cyber hygiene." Perhaps the best example is that the most popular password in use today is "123456," with "password" No. 2.

The 19th century poet Ralph Waldo Emerson never could have conceived of the Internet. But it is what allowed me recently to look up a quote by him that is perhaps the best guide for our age of cyber insecurity: "Knowledge is the antidote to fear."

Online Sexual Predators Are Not a Serious Problem

danah boyd

danah boyd, who signs her name all lowercase, is a principal researcher at Microsoft Research, the founder of Data & Society Research Institute, and the author of the book It's Complicated: The Social Lives of Networked Teens.

If you're a parent, you've probably seen the creepy portraits of online sexual predators constructed by media: The twisted older man, lurking online, ready to abduct a naive and innocent child and do horrible things. If you're like most parents, the mere mention of online sexual predators sends shivers down your spine. Perhaps it prompts you to hover over your child's shoulder or rally your school to host online safety assemblies.

But what if the sexual predator image you have in your mind is wrong? And what if that inaccurate portrait is actually destructive?

The Facts About Sexual Victimization

When it comes to child safety, the real statistics don't stop parental worry. Exceptions dominate the mind. The facts highlight how we fail to protect those teenagers who are most at-risk for sexual exploitation online.

If you poke around, you may learn that 1 in 7 children are sexually exploited online. This data comes from the very reputable Crimes Against Children Research Center, however, very few take the time to read the report carefully. Most children are sexually solicited by their classmates, peers, or young adults just a few years older than they are. And most of these sexual solicitations don't upset teens. Alarm bells should go off over the tiny percentage of youth who are upsettingly solicited by people who are much older than them. No victimization is acceptable, but we need to drill into understanding who is at risk and why if we want to intervene.

Far too many young people are raped and sexually victimized in this country. Only a minuscule number of them are harmed at the hands of strangers, online or off.

The same phenomenal research group, led by David Finkelhor, went on to analyze the recorded cases of sexual victimization linked to the internet and identified a disturbing pattern. These encounters weren't random. Rather, those who were victimized were significantly more likely to be from abusive homes, grappling with addiction or mental health issues, and/or struggling with sexual identity. Furthermore, the recorded incidents showed a more upsetting dynamic. By and large, these youth portrayed themselves as older online, sought out interactions with older men, talked about sex online with these men, met up knowing that sex was in the cards, and did so repeatedly because they believed that they were in love. These teenagers are being victimized, but the go-to solutions of empowering parents, educating youth about strangers, or verifying the age of adults won't put a dent into the issue. These youth need professional help. We need to think about how to identify and support those at-risk, not build another ad campaign.

The Obsession with Sexual Predators

What makes our national obsession with sexual predation destructive is that it is used to justify systematically excluding young people from public life, both online and off. Stopping children from connecting to strangers is seen as critical for their own protection, even though learning to navigate strangers is a key part of growing up. Youth are discouraged from lingering in public parks or navigating malls without parental supervision. They don't learn how to respectfully and conscientiously navigate new people because they are taught to fear all who are unknown.

The other problem with our obsession with sexual predators is that it distracts parents and educators. Everyone rallies to teach children to look out for and fear rare dangers without giving them the tools for managing more common forms of harm that they might encounter. Far too many young people are raped and sexually victimized in this country. Only a minuscule number of them are harmed at the hands of strangers, online or off. Most who will be abused will suffer at the hands of their classmates and peers.

In a culture of abstinence-only education, schools don't want to address any aspect of sexual and reproductive health for fear of upsetting parents. As a result, we fail to give young people the tools to handle sexual victimization. When the message is "just say no," we shame young people who were sexually abused or violated.

It's high time that we walk away from our nightmare scenarios and focus on addressing the serious injustices that exist. The world we live in isn't fair and many youth who are most at-risk do not have concerned parents looking out for them. Because we have stopped raising children as a community, adults are often too afraid to step on other parents' toes. Yet, we need adults who are looking out for more than just their children. Furthermore, our children need us to talk candidly about sexual victimization without resorting to boogeymen.

While it's important to protect youth from dangers, a society based on fear-mongering is not healthy. Let's instead talk about how we can help teenagers be passionate, engaged, constructive members of society rather than how we can protect them from statistically anomalous dangers. Let's understand those teens who are truly at risk; these teens often have the least support.

CHAPTER 3

How Should US Cybersecurity Be Improved?

Overview: Cybersecurity Issues and Challenges

Eric A. Fischer

Eric A. Fischer is the senior specialist in science and technology at the Congressional Research Service of the Library of Congress.

The information technology (IT) industry has evolved greatly over the last half century. Continued, exponential progress in processing power and memory capacity has made IT hardware not only faster, but also smaller, light[er], cheaper, and easier to use.

The original IT industry has also increasingly converged with the communications industry into a combined sector commonly called information and communications technology (ICT). This technology is ubiquitous and increasingly integral to almost every facet of modern society. ICT devices and components are generally interdependent, and disruption of one may affect many others.

The Concept of Cybersecurity

Over the past several years, experts and policy makers have expressed increasing concerns about protecting ICT systems from *cyberattacks*—deliberate attempts by unauthorized persons to access ICT systems, usually with the goal of theft, disruption, damage, or other unlawful actions. Many experts expect the number and severity of cyberattacks to increase over the next several years.

Eric A. Fischer, "Cybersecurity Issues and Challenges: In Brief," *CRS Report*, R43831, Congressional Research Service, December 16, 2014, pp. 1–3. Courtesy of Congressional Research Service.

The act of protecting ICT systems and their contents has come to be known as *cybersecurity*. A broad and arguably somewhat fuzzy concept, cybersecurity can be a useful term but tends to defy precise definition. It usually refers to one or more of three things:

- A set of activities and other measures intended to protect—from attack, disruption, or other threats—computers, computer networks, related hardware and devices software, and the information they contain and communicate, including software and data, as well as other elements of cyberspace.

- The state or quality of being protected from such threats.

- The broad field of endeavor aimed at implementing and improving those activities and quality.

Cybersecurity is . . . sometimes conflated inappropriately in public discussion with other concepts such as privacy, information sharing, intelligence gathering, and surveillance.

It is related to but not generally regarded as identical to the concept of *information security*, which is defined in federal law (44 U.S.C. §3542(b)(1)) as

protecting information and information systems from unauthorized access, use, disclosure, disruption, modification, or destruction in order to provide—

(A) integrity, which means guarding against improper information modification or destruction, and includes ensuring information nonrepudiation and authenticity;

(B) confidentiality, which means preserving authorized restrictions on access and disclosure, including means for protecting personal privacy and proprietary information; and

(C) availability, which means ensuring timely and reliable access to and use of information.

Cybersecurity is also sometimes conflated inappropriately in public discussion with other concepts such as privacy, information sharing, intelligence gathering, and surveillance. Privacy is associated with the ability of an individual person to control access by others to information about that person. Thus, good cybersecurity can help protect privacy in an electronic environment, but information that is shared to assist in cybersecurity efforts might sometimes contain personal information that at least some observers would regard as private. Cybersecurity can be a means of protecting against undesired surveillance of and gathering of intelligence from an information system. However, when aimed at potential sources of cyberattacks, such activities can also be useful to help effect cybersecurity. In addition, surveillance in the form of monitoring of information flow within a system can be an important component of cybersecurity.

Management of Cybersecurity Risks

The risks associated with any attack depend on three factors: *threats* (who is attacking), *vulnerabilities* (how they are attacking), and *impacts* (what the attack does). The management of risk to information systems is considered fundamental to effective cybersecurity.

A successful attack can compromise the confidentiality, integrity, and availability of an ICT system and the information it handles.

What Are the Threats? People who perform cyberattacks generally fall into one or more of five categories: *criminals* intent on monetary gain from crimes such as theft or extortion; *spies* intent on stealing classified or proprietary information used by government or private entities; *nation-state warriors* who develop capabilities and undertake cyberattacks in support of a country's strategic objectives; *"hacktivists"* who perform cyberattacks for nonmonetary reasons; and *terrorists* who engage in cyberattacks as a form of non-state or state-sponsored warfare.

What Are the Vulnerabilities? Cybersecurity is in many ways an arms race between attackers and defenders. ICT systems are very complex, and attackers are constantly probing for weaknesses, which can occur at many points. Defenders can often protect against weaknesses, but three are particularly challenging: inadvertent or intentional acts by *insiders* with access to a system; *supply chain* vulnerabilities, which can permit the insertion of malicious software or hardware during the acquisition process; and previously unknown, or *zero-day*, vulnerabilities with no established fix.

What Are the Impacts? A successful attack can compromise the confidentiality, integrity, and availability of an ICT system and the information it handles. *Cybertheft* or *cyberespionage* can result in exfiltration of financial, proprietary, or personal information from which the attacker can benefit, often without the knowledge of the victim. *Denial-of-service* attacks can slow or prevent legitimate users from accessing a system. *Botnet* malware can give an attacker command of a system for use in cyberattacks on other systems. Attacks on *industrial control systems* can result in the destruction of the equipment they control, such as generators, pumps, and centrifuges.

Most cyberattacks have limited impacts, but a successful attack on some components of critical infrastructure (CI)—most of which is held by the private sector—could have significant effects on national security, the economy, and the livelihood and safety of individual citizens. Thus, a rare successful attack with high impact can pose a larger risk than a common successful attack with low impact.

Reducing the risks from cyberattacks usually involves (1) removing the threat source (e.g., by closing down botnets or reducing incentives for cybercriminals); (2) addressing vulnerabilities by hardening ICT assets (e.g., by patching software and training employees); and (3) lessening impacts by mitigating damage and restoring functions (e.g., by having back-up resources available for continuity of operations in response to an attack).

The federal role in cybersecurity involves both securing federal systems and assisting in protecting nonfederal systems. Under current law, all federal agencies have cybersecurity responsibilities relating to their own systems, and many have sector-specific responsibilities for CI. More than 50 statutes address various aspects of cybersecurity, and new legislation has been debated since at least the 111th Congress. However, until the end of the 113th Congress, no bills on cybersecurity had been enacted since the Federal Information Security Management Act (FISMA) in 2002.

An International Approach Is Needed to Combat Cybercrime

Shavit Matias

Shavit Matias is a research fellow at the Hoover Institution and a member of the Jean Perkins Task Force on National Security and Law.

The cyberattack late last year [2014] on Sony Pictures, intended to deter the release of the movie *The Interview*—combined with threats of physical harm to civilians—threw once again into sharp relief the complexity and dangers of cyberspace. As the heated exchanges between Washington and Pyongyang continue, the weaknesses in cyber defense of private companies and states is again evident, not only in repelling the attack, but in identifying the hackers as well.

The Sony attack is far from a solitary occurrence. Beyond the already well-known cybercrime and cyber espionage phenomena, a dangerous and complex realm is emerging where the level of sophistication of terror groups and states is growing. Cyberterrorism and cyberwarfare have become a key national security threat.

The Rise in Cyberwarfare Capabilities

By way of some examples, in September 2014, various news outlets reported that jihadists in the Middle East, including leaders from both the Islamic State (also known as ISIS) and al Qaeda, were actively planning cyberterror attacks against Western countries, specifically targeting government servers and critical infrastructure. It was further reported that ISIS

Shavit Matias, "Combating Cyberattacks In The Age Of Globalization," hoover.org, *The Briefing*, March 5, 2015. Copyright © 2015 by the Board of Trustees of Leland Stanford Junior University. All rights reserved. Reproduced with permission.

was planning to establish a "cyber caliphate" "intending to mount catastrophic hacking and virus attacks on America and the West." According to Fox News,

> ". . . the terror groups are trying to add to their numbers to boost their capabilities, using social media to reach a larger pool of potential recruits and calling on militant-minded specialists to join them. The targets are the websites of US government agencies, banks, energy companies and transport systems. Islamic State's efforts are spearheaded by a British hacker known as Abu Hussain al Britani, whose real name is Junaid Hussein. He fled his hometown of Birmingham for Syria a year ago to join the group and US intelligence sources say he is one of several key recruiters. Al Britani once led a group of teenage British hackers called Team Poison, and now actively calls for computer-literate jihadists to come to Syria and Iraq."

Iran and North Korea are heavily investing in cyberwarfare capabilities, building as part of their military establishment sophisticated cyber units with defensive and offensive capabilities. A 22-page analysis of Iranian cyberwarfare capabilities published in August [2014] by Israel's Institute for National Security Studies concludes that during the course of 2013, Iran became one of the key players in the international cyberwarfare theater, and points to the many major qualitative and quantitative investments by Iran in this field. The paper outlines cyberattacks conducted by Iran, including a relatively recent large-scale attack on the websites of key banks and financial institutions in the United States, stating that "information security experts described this attack as 'unprecedented in scope and effectiveness.'" Israel has also attributed to Iran numerous cyberattack attempts.

A July 7, 2014 article in *Security Affairs* reports that North Korea doubled the number of units of its cyber army (now estimated to employ approximately 6,000 people), has established overseas bases for hacking attacks, and "is massive[ly] training its young prodigies to become professional hackers." According to the article, "the North Korean cyber army has already hit many times the infrastructure of South Korea, banks, military entities, media and TV broadcasters with malware and other sophisticated techniques."

Russia and China have also heavily invested in such capabilities, and it is reported that their specialized cyberwarfare units are behind several instances of network disruption, technology theft and other cyberattacks against governments and companies. On February 4, 2014, the website tripwire.com reported that "Russian government officials have announced they intend to create a designated military unit devoted to preventing cyber-based attacks from disrupting vital systems devoted to Russian military operations" and that the new unit is expected to be fully operational by 2017.

Over the past decade . . . there has been an increasing focus of industry and states on building tools to enhance capabilities to combat cybercrime, cyber espionage, cyberterrorism and cyberwarfare.

In March of 2014 it was reported that the Latvian army had hired the country's first 13 cyber guards as part of a newly created cyber defense unit.

The Creation of Defense Systems

In a 2012 speech on cybersecurity, then-FBI Director Robert Mueller stated that: "Terrorism remains the FBI's top priority. But in the not-too-distant future, we anticipate that the cyber threat will pose the number one threat to our country." Former US Secretary of Defense Leon Panetta and former director of the NSA [National Security Agency] Keith Alexander have repeatedly warned against a future "cyber Pearl Harbor."

Similarly, the US Department of Defense's 2014 Quadrennial Defense Review declares:

"The Joint Force must also be prepared to battle increasingly sophisticated adversaries who could employ advanced warfighting capabilities while simultaneously attempting to deny US forces the advantages they currently enjoy in space and cyberspace. We will sustain priority investments in science, technology, research, and development both within the defense sector and beyond.[. . .] Innovation is paramount given the increasingly complex warfighting environment we expect to encounter."

Over the past decade, facing the alarming growth of cyberattacks on industry, media, banks, infrastructure and state institutions, there has been an increasing focus of industry and states on building tools to enhance capabilities to combat cybercrime, cyber espionage, cyberterrorism and cyberwarfare, and there is a major shift of funds, efforts, and focus to these areas. Many countries are creating cyber defense institutions within their national security establishments and enhancing their cyber capabilities, including through the creation of dedicated cyberwarfare units within their defense forces. Others are beginning to be aware of the necessity. According to Director of National Intelligence James R. Clapper in a January 29, 2014 Statement for the Record before the Senate Select Committee on Intelligence, the United States estimates that several of the cyber defense institutions created by states will likely be responsible for offensive cyber operations as well.

Israel has been at the forefront of building defenses from cyberattacks—and it too has gone public with its establishment of cyberwarfare units.

The cyber arena is complex and continuously evolving. Recognizing the critical interlink between the various actors and the need for cooperation and innovation, states are increasingly trying to build cooperation between domestic state cyber institutions and industry and academia, and devise mechanisms for internal cooperation between different state units and agencies. While in the past states kept many of these efforts—including information on the formation of military cyber units—relatively secret, today they increasingly publicize their efforts both nationally and internationally.

"Be an Army hacker: This top secret cyber unit wants you" shouts the headline of an April 6, 2013 article in the *Military Times*, explaining that the US Army is looking for computer-savvy American troops to "turn into crack cyberwarriors" for both offensive and defensive purposes. The United States Cyber Command has already announced that over the next few years it intends to recruit 6,000 cyber experts and create teams of soldiers and civilians to assist the Pentagon in defending US national infrastructure.

The United Kingdom is also going public with its efforts. A new cyber unit called the Joint Cyber Reserve has been set up by the Ministry of Defence to help protect critical computer networks from attack, and former Defence Secretary Philip Hammond appealed to Britain's top IT experts to join up and work as military reservists.

Israel has been at the forefront of building defenses from cyberattacks—and it too has gone public with its establishment of cyberwarfare units. According to a November 14, 2013 article in the Israeli newspaper *Haaretz*, the Israeli military has been "bullish" on the cyber front—not only creating sophisticated cyber units but actively involved in "raising the next generation of cyber geeks" through after-school programs and other initiatives geared at preparing today's youth to fight this new kind of war. This is in addition to the establishment of a new national cyber defense authority in conjunction with the Israeli National Cyber Bureau.

A Real Threat

As early as 2011, a study on cybersecurity and cyberwarfare conducted by the Center for Strategic and International Studies (CSIS) had already identified 33 states that include cyberwarfare in their military planning and organization. According to the report, "Common elements in military doctrine include the use of cyber capabilities for reconnaissance, information operations, the disruption of critical networks and services, for 'cyberattacks,' and as a complement to electronic warfare and information operations. Some states include specific plans for informational and political operations. Others link cyberwarfare capabilities with existing electronic warfare planning." The report also points out that in another 36 states, civilian agencies charged with internal security missions, computer security, or law enforcement are also responsible for cybersecurity.

The threat is real and omnipresent. While some states are well into building up their capabilities, others are beginning, and there are those that have not even begun.

The cutting edge for military organizations, the CSIS report explains, is the creation of specific commands dedicated to cyberwarfare, similar to the United States Cyber Command created in 2009. At the time of the 2011 study, CSIS found that 12 states—including North Korea, Denmark, Germany, India, Iran, and South Korea—had established or were planning to establish similar commands. It is likely that other states, such as Cuba and the Russian Federation, will or are developing such organizations as well.

So the cyber swords are sharpened and drawn and have indeed already struck. Western countries spend substantial funds to train and employ many personnel in military establishments, defense establishments, universities, industry, and elsewhere to defend against cybercrime, cyberterrorism, cyberwarfare, and industry attacks, as well as building up their offensive capabilities.

Importantly, and as an additional challenge, these states will have to devise the correct balance between the need to confront these cyber phenomena and the privacy rights of citizens, as the United States has discovered in the wake of the [Eric] Snowden affair. States that have until now taken a very strict view of privacy, particularly in the European Union, are now coping with difficult privacy questions in light of an increasing amount of terrorist attacks and a new phenomenon where it is has been estimated that 5,000 of their own young citizens have joined ISIS, which itself uses cyberspace and social media heavily to recruit as well as to make public their deadly activities. These European recruits may be operating against their home states, and may return to Europe and conduct terrorist attacks there, yet until recently they were undetected.

The threat is real and omnipresent. While some states are well into building up their capabilities, others are beginning, and there are those that have not even begun.

A Global Issue

But whatever stage of preparation a state is in, given the realities of the age of globalization, it is unlikely the solution to national security cyber threats will be found by states trying to act on their own, no matter how sophisticated their internal mechanisms, protections, or armies may be. As states are grappling with their own internal organization, their legal questions (under both domestic and international law), and building their capabilities, they must also look—much sooner than later—to the international front and the challenges it poses to their national security interests.

Cyberterrorism, cyberwarfare and cybercrime are globalized phenomena cutting at light speed across borders, and are committed by attackers who are often difficult to locate and even sometimes impossible to identify. Combating the cyber criminals and terrorists, as well as cyber military units, will require not only strong domestic infrastructure and capabilities, but also similarly strong capabilities and infrastructure in other like-minded states and robust cooperation mechanisms between states and their various institutions, intelligence agencies, and militaries. Cybercrime, cyberwarfare and cyberterrorism can hit national security as well as other interests of a state from places where, without international cooperation, a state has little or no control, nor will it have, without international cooperation, sufficient ability to defend or protect itself.

While there have been some efforts in different international forums to address the issue [of cyberwarfare] . . . to date these efforts have had limited impact.

Furthermore, globalization, and the link between countries and economies, creates many national security interests well beyond state borders. A major attack on the critical infrastructure or military operations of a NATO [North Atlantic Treaty Organization] state in a way that falls under NATO Article 5 is one example. A major attack on offshore branches of US companies or banks in a way that will critically affect the US economy, or an electronic takeover of air command of airports in different areas of the world are others. The scenarios are almost unlimited.

It is not unlikely that the terrorists or states wanting to attack a particular state or business using cyberterrorism or cyberwarfare will look for the weakest links in the global chain and hit wherever they can to harm their primary target.

The Need for an International Effort

The creation of a global action strategic plan in that regard must be a priority. International standards and norms—including enforcement mechanisms—to be applied across the board by states, and mechanisms for information sharing and cooperation, must be put in place sooner rather than later.

While there have been some efforts in different international forums to address the issue—for example, various UN [United Nations] groups of government experts have been convening over the last few years in an effort to achieve consensus and common understandings on the norms that apply with respect to cybersecurity—to date these efforts have had limited impact. Many times, debates on form supplant debates on substance, and progress, if made, is slow. NATO members are making some moves in a cooperative direction, whether in building some capabilities for cooperation between NATO members or examining the relevant international law with the assistance of the impressive Tallinn manual, and there are some efforts in assisting weaker states to strengthen their capabilities, but this too is only a first step.

In order to address the mounting cyber challenges ahead, weaker states, whether NATO members or not, will need assistance in building up their capabilities. Domestic standards, laws, and institutions for combating cybercrime, cyberterrorism and cyberwarfare will need to be put in place. International legal parameters will need to be defined and significant mechanisms for information sharing and cooperation will need to be created.

This will not be an easy venture. There is and will likely be much political and other opposition from states, as well as concerns over information sharing. The challenge is all the more daunting in light of the diametrically opposed views of the United States and other Western countries, on the one hand, and Russia and China on the other, regarding the manner in which cyberspace should be regulated. But while states are struggling with legal and other definitions, and debating their differences, terror organizations are forging right ahead as are unfriendly cyber armies. Time is not on the side of the Western nations, nor is it on the side of their private domestic industry and businesses that are many times the targets of the cyberattacks.

A concentrated effort is needed to try to close this serious gap in security. Lessons learnt from other international efforts—such as mechanisms and standards put in place to combat terrorism, money laundering, organized crime, trafficking in persons, or corruption—can be examined and, where applicable, could perhaps be followed and expanded and elaborated upon to meet the different needs arising from the serious and dangerous cyber challenge. Although devising international instruments and mechanisms for the cyber threat is likely much more complex, for a range of reasons, these examples interlinking trade interests, blacklists, sanctions, diplomatic pressure, and other measures with the creation of domestic and international standards and instruments have assisted to an extent in combating these cross-border phenomena.

These examples, which include also the creation of certain mechanisms for cooperation and information sharing, standards for industry, as well as other standards, show that in the age of globalization not only is it necessary to create the norms and infrastructure for states to work together to combat cross-border issues, but it may also be more possible to persuade states to do so if a strong lead is taken, whether by one powerful state or a group of states. Compelling measures must be put in place making it in the direct interests of states and industry to cooperate and adopt standards and cooperation methodologies.

Cyberterrorism, cybercrime and cyberwarfare pose a real and significant threat to national security. Together with increasing domestic efforts, it is time for strong operation on the international front.

Stuxnet and the Dangers of Cyberwar

Vincent Manzo

Vincent Manzo is a fellow in the Defense and National Security Group at the Center for Strategic and International Studies' International Security Program.

Operation Olympic Games, more commonly known as the Stuxnet worm, damaged Iran's centrifuges and delayed its uranium enrichment efforts. As David Sanger reports in *Confront and Conceal*, President Obama expressed concern about collateral damage in the U.S.-Israeli cyber attack on Iran's nuclear program. The president didn't want to set a precedent that would enable other actors to justify similar cyber attacks. But he concluded that the need to delay Iran's progress toward a nuclear-weapons capability was worth the risk in this instance, while his national-security team judged that it was too early to develop a conceptual framework for evaluating the use of cyber weapons.

Despite the administration's decision to grapple with broader policy issues later, Stuxnet raises fundamental questions about cyber weapons. The United States authorized the operation in peacetime rather than in an armed conflict. Yet the operation fits the definition of a cyber attack, an attempt to destroy, degrade, or alter systems, typically to cause a secondary effect in the physical world. The United States manipulated Iranian computer systems to physically damage Iranian infrastructure. The operation was thus more than cyber exploitation, which covertly mines information from networks without authorization.

Many believe Iran is responsible for a wave of denial of service attacks on U.S. banks, though it is unclear if that was retaliation for Stuxnet, assassinations of Iranian scientists, other perceived offenses, or part of Iran's consistently belligerent behavior. Setting aside the complexities of U.S.-Iranian relations, Sanger's reporting illuminates dangers associated with cyber attacks that U.S. policy must address.

Stuxnet does not prove that cyber attacks are low-risk operations. Rather, it suggests that the effects, and thus the risks, of cyber attacks are unpredictable.

The physical effects of the operation were limited to covertly disabling Iranian centrifuges. U.S. and Israeli officials sought to slow down Iran's enrichment program and confuse scientists without revealing that an attack was underway. They introduced variants of the worm into Iranian facilities over a period of several years, only after reconnaissance operations gathered intelligence about Iranian facilities, operations, and computer networks. Engineers then refined the worm by testing it on U.S. replicas of Iran's Natanz enrichment facility. As an operation that was highly sophisticated, requiring large investments of time and resources, an emphasis on concealment, multiple strikes, and limited physical effects rather than large-scale destruction, Stuxnet was closer to sabotage than a full military attack.

That the United States and Israel executed this plan is astounding, though Stuxnet failed to satisfy its own standards of success in one regard: according to Sanger, the worm was never intended to travel outside Natanz's isolated, air-gapped networks. But an error in the code caused the worm to replicate itself and spread when an Iranian technician connected an infected laptop computer to the internet. Fortunately, the worm did not cause widespread damage because it was engineered to affect Iranian enrichment facilities only; however, Stuxnet's unauthorized globetrotting evokes several nightmare scenarios.

Imagine if the Stuxnet worm caused far more destruction than expected. Would Iran have retaliated via terrorist attacks or conventional weapons? Would widespread damage to Iranian civilian infrastructure have weakened international support for sanctions? How would other countries have reacted if Stuxnet damaged their infrastructure, especially once they discovered who created the worm? Each of these outcomes would have undermined U.S. strategic objectives and triggered unforeseen problems.

Efforts to customize future attacks to specific targets and calibrate their precise effects might fail. Given these uncertainties, cyber weapons appear to be a niche capability. Their use may be justified in a handful of scenarios. In fact, Sanger reports that the United States moved forward with Stuxnet because it was a safer alternative to conventional strikes. Yet Stuxnet does not prove that cyber attacks are low-risk operations. Rather, it suggests that the effects, and thus the risks, of cyber attacks are unpredictable. Thus Stuxnet should instill caution in U.S. operations as much as it boosts confidence.

But U.S. policy for using cyber weapons is only part of the equation. How other countries wield cyber weapons will affect the United States as well. Vulnerable computer networks and systems support U.S. economic activities, military capabilities, and societal services such as critical infrastructure. Just as U.S. officials concluded the effects and risks of the Stuxnet operation were proportionate to the payoffs, other countries might reach similar conclusions about cyber attacks against the United States. Improving cyber defenses, attribution capabilities, and developing credible retaliatory options will play an important role in deterring and mitigating direct cyber attacks, but cascading viruses launched at other countries could eventually penetrate and damage U.S. networks.

The United States failed to prevent the Stuxnet worm from escaping an air-gapped system. What if countries, terrorist organizations, or even business competitors with less-discriminating cyber weapons, and perhaps less caution, start launching attacks or view cyber weapons as an acceptable tool for the day-to-day disagreements that dominate international politics? Defense and deterrence alone are insufficient for coping with the staggering number of actors and threats in cyberspace. The United States should work to influence how and how often other countries launch cyber attacks.

The United States could explain its criteria and process for evaluating a cyber attack's risks of unintended and unanticipated damage.

For now, greater transparency about U.S. policies governing the use of cyber weapons is a modest and practical approach to establishing international norms for cyber attacks. The United States could articulate a narrative about how it conducts cyber attacks, why, and against what types of countries and targets. U.S. officials must answer these questions to develop a doctrine for the effective use of cyber weapons in any case.

The United States could explain its criteria and process for evaluating a cyber attack's risks of unintended and unanticipated damage. Is there a task force that provides an independent "red team" risk assessment of potential operations? Is there a higher threshold for attacks on targets connected to the internet? Is there a testing process for new cyber weapons? Do all cyber attacks require presidential authorization? Explaining how the United States applies the law of armed conflict to cyber attacks, rather than simply asserting that the law applies, would set a powerful example. Some countries might not care, but others might impose similarly strict standards on their own operations. At the very least, U.S. officials would have credibility when advocating for tacit or nonbinding standards of conduct in cyberspace.

Explaining the purposes for which the United States would use cyber weapons in peacetime is another challenge facing U.S. officials. For example, an alleged cyber attack unleashed a persistent virus that erased data on Iranian Oil Ministry hard disks. This attack employed a cyber weapon to hinder Iran's oil exports, perhaps to pressure it into making concessions on its nuclear program. There is no evidence that the United States is responsible.

But it is unclear if U.S. policy considers this a legitimate use of cyber weapons, and many other questions remain. Is there a meaningful distinction between sabotaging WMD-related programs and attacking a country's economic vitality to compel it to abandon those programs? Where might the United States show restraint? Are networks supporting critical civilian infrastructure (assuming Iran's centrifuges are not for peaceful purposes) acceptable targets?

It might also be that peacetime attacks are reserved solely for countries with illicit military programs. For example, U.S. nuclear declaratory policy rules out the use of nuclear weapons against non-nuclear weapon states that are in compliance with their non-proliferation obligations. Perhaps the United States could pledge to refrain from Stuxnet-style attacks against countries that can verify that they will forgo nuclear, chemical and biological weapons programs.

If absolute prohibitions are too constraining, the United States could establish reciprocal limits on the use of cyber weapons on a country-by-country basis. In *The Paradox of Power*, David Gompert and Phillip Saunders analyze the prospects for a U.S.-China strategic restraint regime. Both countries would refrain from launching cyber attacks on each other's economic and civilian networks. Because both countries depend on these vulnerable networks and are capable of retaliating, mutual deterrence in this specific context is feasible. Rather than foreswearing attacks on tactical military networks, U.S. and Chinese officials would acknowledge that such attacks carry unique risks of escalation and require authorization at the highest levels of the government. This is a promising approach to developing norms in a domain characterized by anonymity and unlimited actors. There is always emphasis on rogue actors beyond the control of states. But the United States, China, and other major powers can control their own use of destructive cyber weapons and have a shared interest in clarifying boundaries.

With so much uncertainty about how cyber weapons will evolve, U.S. officials might be tempted to hold off on public explanations of policy, deliberate in secret, and maintain flexibility. But if U.S. vulnerability in cyberspace persists, an international consensus on minimizing collateral damage, avoiding attacks on civilian targets and stigmatizing coercive peacetime attacks would serve the national interest. Establishing principles to guide U.S. use of cyber weapons and explaining them to the world is a prudent first step.

Official silence is not the same as saying nothing. Consider some of the headlines from the *Washington Post*: "Pentagon Ups Ante on Cyber Front;" "Cyberweapons on Pentagon Fast Track;" "U.S. Builds a Cyber Plan X." These articles signal that the United States will have a first-rate suite of offensive cyber capabilities. It is time for Washington to show that it is also crafting a prudent doctrine to govern their use.

Ethical Questions Need to Be Answered About Cyberweapons

Patrick Lin, Fritz Allhoff, and Neil Rowe

Patrick Lin is the director of the Ethics + Emerging Sciences Group based in the philosophy department at California Polytechnic State University, San Luis Obispo. Fritz Allhoff is an associate philosophy professor at Western Michigan University and a senior research fellow at Australia's Centre for Applied Philosophy and Public Ethics. Neil Rowe is a professor of computer science at the US Naval Postgraduate School.

In the last week or so [May/June 2012], cyberwarfare has made front-page news: the United States may have been behind the Stuxnet cyberattack on Iran; Iran may have suffered another digital attack with the Flame virus; and our military and industrial computer chips may or may not be compromised by backdoor switches implanted by China. These revelations suggest that the way we fight wars is changing, and so are the rules.

This digital evolution means that it is now less clear what kind of events should reasonably trigger a war, as well as how and when new technologies may be used. With cyberweapons, a war theoretically could be waged without casualties or political risk, so their attractiveness is great—maybe so irresistible that nations are tempted to use them before such aggression is justified. This essay identifies some important ethical issues that have been upturned by these emerging digital weapons, which in turn help explain why national cyberdefense is such a difficult policy area.

Patrick Lin, Fritz Allhoff, and Neil Rowe, "Is It Possible to Wage a Just Cyberwar?," *Atlantic*, June 5, 2012. Copyright © 2012 Atlantic Monthly Group. All rights reserved. Reproduced with permission.

The Laws of Cyberwar

How we justify and prosecute a war matters. For instance, the last U.S. presidency proposed a doctrine of preventive or pre-emptive war, known as the "Bush doctrine," which asked, if a nation knows it will be attacked, why wait for the damage to be done before it retaliates? But this policy breaks from the just-war tradition, which historically gives moral permission for a nation to enter war only in self-defense. This tradition says that waging war—a terrible evil that is to be avoided when possible—requires a nation to have the righteous reason of protecting itself from further unprovoked attacks.

Our world is increasingly wired, with new online channels for communication and services interwoven into our lives virtually every day. This also means new channels for warfare.

With the Bush doctrine, the U.S. seeks to expand the triggers for war—and this could backfire spectacularly. For instance, Iran reports contemplating a preemptive attack on the U.S. and Israel, because it believes that one or both will attack Iran first. Because intentions between nations are easy to misread, especially between radically different cultures and during an election year, it could very well be that the U.S. and Israel are merely posturing as a gambit to pressure Iran to open its nuclear program to international inspection. However, if Iran were to attack first, it would seem hypocritical for the U.S. to complain, since the U.S. already endorsed the same policy of first strike.

A big problem with a first-strike policy is that there are few scenarios in which we can confidently and accurately say that an attack is imminent. Many threats or bluffs that were never intended to escalate into armed conflict can be mistaken as "imminent" attacks. This epistemic gap in the Bush doctrine introduces a potentially catastrophic risk: The nation delivering a preemptive or preventative first strike may turn out to be the unjustified aggressor and not the would-be victim, if the adversary really was not going to attack first.

Further, by not saving war as a last resort—after all negotiations have failed and after an actual attack, a clear act of war—the Bush doctrine opens the possibility that the U.S. (and any other nation that adopts such a policy) may become ensnared in avoidable wars. At the least, this would cause harm that otherwise might not have occurred to the warring parties, and it may set up an overly stretched military for failure, if battles are not chosen more wisely.

What does this have to do with cyberwarfare? Our world is increasingly wired, with new online channels for communication and services interwoven into our lives virtually every day. This also means new channels for warfare. Indeed, a target in cyberspace is more appealing than conventional physical targets, since the aggressor would not need to incur the expense and risk of transporting equipment and deploying troops across borders into enemy territory, not to mention the political risk of casualties. Cyberweapons could be used to attack anonymously at a distance while still causing much mayhem, on targets ranging from banks to media to military organizations. Thus, cyberweapons would seem to be an excellent choice for an unprovoked surprise strike.

Today, many nations have the capability to strike in cyberspace—but should they? International humanitarian laws, or the "laws of war," were not written with cyberspace in mind. So we face a large policy gap, which organizations internationally have tried to address in recent years, such as the U.S. National Research Council. But there is also a gap in developing the ethics behind policies. We describe below some key issues related to ethics that need attention.

One Just Cause for War

By the laws of war, there is historically only one "just cause" for war: a defense to aggression, as previously mentioned. But since aggression is usually understood to mean that human lives are directly in jeopardy, it becomes difficult to justify military response to a cyberattack that does not cause kinetic or physical harm as in a conventional or Clausewitzian [after Prussian military theorist Carl von Clausewitz] sense, such as the disruption of a computer system or infrastructure that directly kills no one. Further, in cyberspace, it may be difficult to distinguish an attack from espionage or vandalism, neither of which historically is enough to trigger a military response. For instance, a clever cyberattack can be subtle and hard to distinguish from routine breakdowns and malfunctions.

Effective cyberattacks need to search for targets and spread the attack, but as with biological viruses, this creates the risk of spreading to noncombatants.

If aggression in cyberspace is not tied to actual physical harm or threat to lives, it is unclear then how we should understand it. Does it count as aggression when malicious software has been installed on a computer system that an adversary believes will be triggered? Or maybe the very act of installing malicious software is an attack itself, much like installing a landmine? What about unsuccessful attempts to install malicious software? Do these count as war-triggering aggression—or mere crimes, which do not fall under the laws of war? Traditional military ethics would answer all these questions negatively, but in the debate over the legitimacy of preemptive and preventative war, the answers are more complex and elusive.

Relatedly, insofar as most cyberattacks do not directly target lives, are they as serious as conventional attacks? Organized cybervandalism could be serious if it prevents a society from meeting basic human needs like providing food. A lesser but still serious case was the denial-of-service cyberattacks on media-infrastructure websites in the country of Georgia in 2008, which prevented the government from communicating with its citizens.

Avoiding Noncombatants

The laws of war prohibit the targeting of noncombatants, since they do not pose a military threat. Most theorists accept a "double effect" in which some noncombatants could be unintentionally harmed, i.e., collateral damage, in pursuing important military objectives, though other scholars defend more stringent requirements and greater protections for noncombatants. Some challenge whether noncombatant immunity is really a preeminent value, but the issue undoubtedly has taken center stage in just-war theory and therefore the laws of war.

It is unclear how discriminatory cyberwarfare can be. If victims use fixed Internet addresses for their key infrastructure systems, and these could be found by an adversary, then they could be targeted precisely. However, victims are unlikely to be so cooperative. Therefore, effective cyberattacks need to search for targets and spread the attack, but as with biological viruses, this creates the risk of spreading to noncombatants: while noncombatants might not be targeted, there are also no safeguards to help avoid them. The Stuxnet worm in 2010 was intended to target Iranian nuclear processing facilities, but it spread far beyond intended targets. Although its damage was highly constrained, its quick, broad infection through vulnerabilities in the Microsoft Windows operating system was noticed and required upgrades to antivirus software worldwide, incurring a cost to nearly everyone. The worm also inspired clever ideas for new exploits currently being used, another cost to everyone. Arguably, then, Stuxnet did incur some collateral damage.

Cyberattackers could presumably appeal to the doctrine of double effect, arguing that effects on noncombatants are acceptable because they are unintended, though foreseen. This may not be plausible, given how precise computers can be when we want. Alternatively, cyberattackers could argue that their attacks were not directly against noncombatants but against infrastructure. However, attacking a human body's immune system, such as the AIDS virus does, can be worse than causing bodily harm directly. Details matter: for instance, if it knocks out electricity and the refrigeration necessary to protect the food supply, even a modest cyberattack could lead to starvation and suffering of innocents.

A possible problem with cyberwarfare is that it is very easy to mask the identities of combatants.

The Principle of Proportionality

Proportionality in just-war theory is the idea that it would be wrong to cause more harm in defending against an attack than the harm of the attack in the first place. This idea comes from utilitarian ethics and is also linked to the notion of fairness in war. For example, a cyberattack that causes little harm should not be answered by a conventional attack that kills hundreds. But as one U.S. official described the nation's cyberstrategy, "If you shut down our power grid, maybe we will put a missile down one of your smokestacks."

A challenge to proportionality is that certain cyberattacks, like biological viruses, might spiral out of control regardless of the attackers' intentions. While those consequences could be tolerated to prevent even worse consequences, lack of control means an attack might not be able to be called off after the victim surrenders, violating another key law of war. Another issue is that the target of a cyberattack may have difficulty assessing how much damage they have received. A single malfunction in software can cause widely varied symptoms; thus a victim may think they have been harmed more than they actually have, motivating a disproportionate counterattack. Therefore, counterattack in cyberspace—a key deterrent to unprovoked attacks—is now fraught with ethical difficulties.

The Principle of Attribution

Discrimination in just-war theory also requires that combatants be identifiable to clarify which targets are legitimate; this is the principle of attribution of attackers and defenders. Terrorism ignores this requirement and therefore elicits moral condemnation. Likewise, a possible problem with cyberwarfare is that it is very easy to mask the identities of combatants. Then counterattack risks hurting innocent victims, if the responsible party is unknown. For example, the lack of attribution of Stuxnet raises ethical concerns because it denied Iran the ability to counterattack, encouraging it towards ever more extreme behavior.

Attribution is not only about moral responsibility but also criminal (or civil) liability: we need to know who to blame and, conversely, who can be absolved of blame. To make attribution work, we need international agreements. We first could agree that cyberattacks should carry a digital signature of the attacking organization. Signatures are easy to compute, and their presence can itself be concealed with the techniques of steganography, so there are no particular technical obstacles to using them. Nation-states could also agree to use networking protocols, such as IPv6, that make attribution easier, and they could cooperate better on international network monitoring to trace sources of attacks. Economic incentives, such as the threat of trade sanctions, can make such agreements desirable.

The Problem with Treacherous Deceit

Perfidy, or deception that abuses the mutual trust needed for fair conduct in warfare, is prohibited by both Hague and Geneva Conventions. For instance, soldiers are not permitted to impersonate humanitarian workers and enemy soldiers. In contrast, some ruses, misinformation, false operations, camouflage, and ambush of combatants are explicitly permissible. Cyberattacks almost inevitably involve an element of deception, such as tricking a user to click on a malicious link. So, to what extent could cyberattacks count as perfidy and therefore be illegal given international humanitarian law? (Consider, for instance, a fake email addressed from the International Committee of the Red Cross to a military organization, but actually sent by some malicious nation-state along with a virus: how is this different from posing as a Red Cross worker?)

The right time to investigate [the ethical issues of cyberwarfare] is prior to the use of cyberweapons, not during an emotional and desperate conflict or after international outcry.

To understand why perfidy is prohibited, we can look at its twin concept of treachery: a prototypical example of a treacherous (and also illegal) act in war is to kill with poison. But why should poison be so categorically banned, given that some poisons can kill quickly and painlessly, much more humanly than a bullet to the head? This apparent paradox suggests that the concept of treachery—and therefore perfidy—is fuzzy and hard to apply. We don't get as angry when software betrays us as when people betray us. But maybe we should. Software would be better if users were less complacent.

A Lasting Peace

In just-war theory, recent attention has focused on the cessation of hostilities and establishment of a lasting peace, given problems with recent insurgencies. The consensus is that combatants have obligations after the conflict is over. For example, an attacking force might be obligated to provide police forces until the attacked state can stabilize, or attackers might have duties to rebuild the damage done by their weaponry.

This suggests that cyberattacks could be morally superior to traditional attacks insofar as they could be engineered to be reversible. When damage done is to data or programs, the originals may be restorable perfectly from backup copies, something that has no analogy with guns and bombs. Sophisticated, responsible attacks could even use encryption to make its reversal a matter of decryption. Such restoration could be done quickly if the attack was narrowly targeted, and it could be done remotely. Therefore, mandating reversal of cyberattacks after hostilities have ceased could even become part of the laws of war. However, reversibility is not guaranteed when it is unclear what is damaged or so much is damaged that restoration takes an unacceptable amount of time. We need to establish ethical norms for reversibility and make them design requirements for cyberattack methods.

The issues sketched above are only some of the basic ethical questions we need to resolve, if national cyberpolicies are to be supported by consistent and reasonable principles. The right time to investigate them is prior to the use of cyberweapons, not during an emotional and desperate conflict or after international outcry. Thinking about ethics after the fact is much less effective. For instance, the Ottawa Treaty prohibits the use of indiscriminate landmines, but countless landmines still lie buried, until someone—perhaps a child—discovers it with his or her life; similarly, the Non-Proliferation Treaty has reduced but not stopped the spread and threat of nuclear weapons.

With cyberweapons, we have the chance to get it right from the start, as we do with other emerging technologies. We need not be helpless bystanders, merely watching events unfold and warfare evolve in the digital age. With hindsight and foresight, we have the power to be proactive. By building ethics into the design and use of cyberweapons, we can help ensure that war is not more cruel than it already is.

Why Aren't We Retaliating Right Now for the Sony Cyberattack?

Yishai Schwartz

Yishai Schwartz is an associate editor at Lawfare.

On Wednesday, Sony cancelled the release of its latest mediocre Seth Rogen comedy, *The Interview*, in the face of terrorism threats from hackers who had been wreaking havoc on the company since late November. Reportedly, American intelligence officials are convinced that the North Korean government was "centrally involved," but they seem paralyzed about how to respond. That alone is upsetting, but even more disturbing is the apparent absence of a readily available doctrine for dealing with attacks of this kind.

This is not the first time a foreign government has targeted American-based companies for political reasons. Earlier this year, a sophisticated cyberattack shut down the computers, phones, email and other technology systems of the Las Vegas Sands Corporation, seriously disrupting the $14 billion operation. Investigators quickly concluded that the attack had originated in Iran, something that experts believe would not have been possible without the cooperation of the governing regime. Given the timing, the attacks were likely motivated by Iranian anger at Sands owner Sheldon Adelson's calls for military action against Iran's nuclear program. But as with Sony, the U.S. government's response was almost entirely passive. As former CIA Director Michael Hayden told *Bloomberg Businessweek*, "If this would have come across my desk when I was in government, I would have just put it in the outbox."

The government's passivity in the face of these cyberat-tacks is not entirely unreasonable. As with other forms of ter-rorism and non-traditional warfare, it is often difficult to trace precisely who is responsible for a cyberattack and the degree of state culpability. And neither slot machines nor Seth Rogen are exactly critical U.S. infrastructure. What's more, cyber-operations inevitably reveal something about our capa-bilities and can swiftly be coopted by our enemies. Elements of the Stuxnet virus (a presumably Israeli creation that suc-cessfully set back Iran's nuclear program by years) have begun cropping up in other cyber-attacks across the globe, as Bruce Schneier, a cyber-security expert affiliated with Harvard's Berkman Center, told me recently.

The only way to prevent future attacks is for foreign gov-ernments to know that attacks against U.S. targets—cyber or kinetic—will bring fierce, yet proportionally ap-propriate, responses.

These concerns are reasons for caution, not an excuse for inaction. The cyberattacks on Sands and Sony have already cost millions, if not billions in property damage, and they have dealt a chilling blow to freedom of expression. It's bad enough that totalitarian regimes control the artistic output of their own countries, but that they could successfully restrict speech in the world's greatest superpower is as bewildering as it is frightening. The entire reason for the existence of a state is the protection of its citizens, especially from foreign threats. If states can no longer play this role then we are well on our way to returning to the state of nature.

It need not be this way. During the Cold War, American strategists developed complex doctrines of multi-layered de-terrence. In the early years, figures like President Dwight Eisen-hower were taken with the idea that nuclear weapons might provide the ultimate deterrent—and that conventional weapons were becoming obsolete. But over time, we learned that nuclear weapons really only deter other nuclear weapons— and that, to avoid unacceptable escalations, conventional Soviet attacks would have to be countered by conventional American responses. To provide a credible threat and effective deterrent, the United States poured resources into developing a full arsenal of graduated, flexible responses, and devoted the time and care into developing a comprehensive strategy that allowed for their swift deployment.

It is past time to do the same for the sphere of cyber-war. Weeks after the initial attacks on Sony, the hemming and hawing and internal White House debate over whether to even publicly identify North Korea as the perpetrator are no longer a sign of caution, but of dithering and poor planning. Some Pentagon shelf is no doubt stocked with contingency plans for various levels of retaliation against various levels of kinetic aggression from unfriendly states. Similar plans should have been developed in the cybersphere years ago, and the president should be prepared to deploy them. The only way to prevent future attacks is for foreign governments to know that attacks against U.S. targets—cyber or kinetic—will bring fierce, yet proportionally appropriate, responses. In order for other governments to know that the U.S. will respond, first our government must know that it will respond.

In a 2012 speech, then-Secretary of Defense Leon Panetta outlined a doctrine of cyber-deterrence that involved retaliation only against those attacks that cause "significant, physical destruction in the United States or kill American citizens." This is no longer enough. Deterrence against large-scale attacks is critical, but so is the everyday security that allows Americans to produce satirical films. Giving up on the latter because it is not quite a "Cyber Pearl Harbor" is an invitation to the slow, steady erosion of basic freedoms that we too often take for granted.

The United States Must Stay on the Offensive for Cybersecurity

James Jay Carafano

James Jay Carafano is the vice president of the Kathryn and Shelby Cullom Davis Institute for National Security and Foreign Policy, and the E.W. Richardson Fellow at The Heritage Foundation.

You know the situation is desperate when debate over how to solve a big problem brings to mind the old wheeze about the weather: Everybody talks about it, but nobody. . . .

And so it goes with cybersecurity. On this issue, Washington resembles a tribe of cavemen (and women) who, 60 years after the invention of the wheel, still gaze upon the tool and ask each other: "What next?"

Offense Without Defense

To be fair, when it comes to military and intelligence applications, Washington has advanced the cybersecurity ball quite well. Our side can do cyberstuff no one in the world can defend against. The problem is, even we can't defend against those advances. That's a worry. If we can take the offensive, so can others.

The dangers lurking in cyberworld made headlines last week [November 2011] with reports of a cyber-attack on a public water utility in Springfield, Ill. Initial news accounts said foreign hackers had inserted malicious software into the pump-control system, causing it to malfunction and burn out. The Department of Homeland Security now says foreign hackers weren't involved. But the incident as originally reported sounded quite like the cyber-attack that infected an Iranian nuclear-fuel production facility with the Stuxnet virus.

Of course, there are no "easy button" answers for cyberdefenses. The online world is one of the most dynamic environments on earth. Technology advances too rapidly to be defended by White House-appointed cyberczars manning the cyber-Maginot Line parapets. As soon as new firewalls and virus-protection programs are fielded, new malicious software and botnets assault them.

All-out cyberwar between major actors such as China and the U.S. is unlikely because that likely would result in mutual cyberdestruction.

For the foreseeable future, then, the most vital work on national cybersecurity will be staying on the offensive and going after the cyber-bad-guys. Hard.

The Need for Cyberdeterrence

Some say it's impossible to get to the bad guys, that it's too difficult to determine where an attack originates because it can be routed through numerous servers and third-party computers around the world. But that argument weakens by the day. Cyberforensics and early-warning systems are being developed and fielded as fast as new threats. Moreover, analyzing Internet traffic isn't the only way to track down bad cyberactors. Good intelligence operations can get the information needed to unmask the bad guys.

In reality, attribution usually is a problem either because the attacks are so numerous and nuanced they're simply not worth running down or because the perpetrators are those we don't want to expose. (Think Russia and China. If Washington publicly admitted they're robbing us blind online, Washington would have to do something about it.)

In the latter instances, a little cyberdeterrence can go a long way. All-out cyberwar between major actors such as China and the U.S. is unlikely because that likely would result in mutual cyberdestruction.

Good Cyber-Counterinsurgency

In addition to investing a lot in cybersecurity, Washington needs to think more broadly about cyberwar. It's not just our electrons fighting their electrons. We must retain the capacity to go after bad cyber-actors with all the instruments of national power—economic, political, diplomatic and military power—not just software.

My Heritage Foundation colleague Paul Rosenzweig insists that we need a fully stocked cybersecurity toolbox. We should view ourselves as fighting a cyber-counterinsurgency, he says, and we need more than cyberbullets to fire back. We also must attack our cyber-enemies' means of financial support, political cover and legal status. Treat them like enemy combatants, criminals, hacktivists and heretics all at the same time, Mr. Rosenzweig says.

The fate of WikiLeaks and its fuzzy-headed founder, Julian Assange, offers a case in point. The organization has been assaulted and spurned by all sides, from companies such as Pay-Pal and Mastercard that cut off its services to the initiators of an armada of legal actions. WikiLeaks is on the brink of collapse.

Most important for the prosecution of good cyber-counterinsurgency: All the instruments of power have to be played as if they are in the same orchestra. That requires a strong, committed conductor.

Cult of the Cyber Offensive

P.W. Singer and Allan Friedman

*P.W. Singer is director of the Center for 21st Century Security
and Intelligence at the Brookings Institution, and Allan Friedman is director of Cybersecurity Initiatives at the National Telecommunications and Information Administration in the US Department of Commerce. They are coauthors of the book*
Cybersecurity and Cyberwar: What Everyone Needs to Know.

In military circles 100 years ago, whatever the question was,
attack was always the answer.

Attaque à outrance, or "Attack to excess," was a concept
that took hold in European military circles at the turn of the
20th century. The idea was that new technologies like the rail-
road and telegraph gave an advantage at the strategic level to
whichever nation could mobilize first and go on the offensive,
while new technologies like the fast-firing cannon, machine
guns, and rifles meant at the tactical level that the troops who
showed the greatest offensive *élan* (a concept that combined
both willpower and dash) would always carry the day on the
battlefield. The philosophy gained huge popularity. In Germany, it drove the adoption of the Schlieffen Plan (which envisioned a rapid mobilization of the army to first knock out
France to its west with a lightning offensive and then swing
back to face Russia to the east), while in France it was actually
written into military law in 1913 that the French army "hence-
forth admits no law but the offensive."

There were only two problems with *Attaque à outrance,* an
idea that historians now call the "cult of the offensive." The
first was that it drove the European powers into greater and
greater competition and ultimately war. When crisis loomed

after the assassination of Archduke Franz Ferdinand in 1914, few thought it worth going to war. But soon the sides feared that they were losing a tight window of opportunity during which to mobilize to their advantage, or even worse, that they would be caught helpless. Fear of being on the defensive prompted the powers to move to the offensive, launching their long-planned attacks as part of a war most didn't want. The second problem was even worse. These new technologies didn't actually give the offense the advantage. Once the war started, it became clear that "attacking to excess" against fast-firing artillery, rifles, and machines guns was not the way to quick victory, but rather to a quick death. A bloody stalemate of trench warfare instead resulted.

The conventional wisdom about offensive advantage has become so entrenched that some argue that the real problem is not that the offense has an advantage, but that it isn't talked about enough.

Today, this question of whether new technology favors offense or defense is a critical one for cybersecurity and cyberwar, and it shapes everything from the likelihood of war to how governments and even businesses should organize themselves. And just as prior to the outbreak of World War I, there is widespread assumption that cyberattack has the inherent advantage over cyberdefense. As one Pentagon-funded report concluded in 2010, "The cyber competition will be offense-dominant for the foreseeable future." This kind of thinking is why Congress repeatedly in 2013 pressed the U.S. military about its cyberoffense capabilities, to make sure we are ahead, with military leaders like Gen. Keith Alexander, the simultaneous head of the NSA and Cyber Command, assuring them that, "Our offense is the best in the world."

This belief in the inherent superiority of cyberoffense has helped drive increased spending on offensive capabilities by militaries around the world, with the U.S. military spending, depending on the measure, 2.5 to 4 times as much on cyber-offense research and development as cyberdefense research. An accompanying industry has also arisen: markets for so-called zero days—coding flaws that can be exploited by hackers—and now even "hackback" firms that will take the offensive for hire.

The conventional wisdom about offensive advantage has become so entrenched that some argue that the real problem is not that the offense has an advantage, but that it isn't talked about enough, meaning that few have been warned about the risks of actually using such weapons. "We've got to step up the game; we've got to talk about our offensive capabilities and train to them; to make them credible so that people know there's a penalty to this," said James Cartwright, the four-star Marine Corps general who led much of the initial U.S. strategy in cyber issues until his retirement in 2011. "You can't have something that's a secret be a deterrent. Because if you don't know it's there, it doesn't scare you." (Two years later, this quote took on far greater resonance, when Cartwright was reported to have been the alleged source of leaks to the media that revealed the U.S. role in building Stuxnet, the first true use of a cyberweapon.)

The basic thinking behind assumed offensive dominance is, as one Center for Strategic and Budgetary Assessments (CSBA) report explained, "It will be cheaper and easier to attack information systems than it will be to detect and defend against attacks." Indeed, as a former senior Pentagon official explained, "A few teenaged hackers sipping Red Bull in their parent's basement can have a WMD-style impact."

More importantly, the attackers have the advantage of being able to choose the time and place of their attack, whereas the defender has to be everywhere. This is true with any weapon, but in cyberspace it is even more pronounced. While in the physical world territory is relatively fixed, the amount of "ground" that the defender has to protect is almost always growing in the cyberworld—and growing exponentially. The number of users on computer networks over time is an almost constant upward curve, while the number of lines of code in security software, measured in the thousands two decades ago, is now well over 10 million. By comparison, malware has stayed relatively short and simple (some is as succinct as just 125 lines of code), and the attacker only has to get in through one node just one time to potentially compromise all the defensive efforts. As the director of the Defense Advanced Research Projects Agency (DARPA), put it, "Cyber defenses have grown exponentially in effort and complexity, but they continue to be defeated by offenses that require far less investment by the attacker."

Stuxnet ended up not just in the Iranian targets, but in thousands of computers around the world, from India to Eastern Europe.

Just as before World War I, however, the story of offense's inherent advantage is actually not so simple. The cyberattacks that are truly dangerous require a great deal of expertise to put together. And while they might play out in terms of microseconds, they often take long periods of planning and intelligence gathering to lay the groundwork. Neither Rome nor Stuxnet was built in a day. This means that crippling attacks out of the blue are not as easy to pull off in the cyber world as is too often depicted by both policymakers and Hollywood.

Another challenge for offensive actors is that the outcome of a cyberattack can be highly uncertain. You may be able to get inside a system or even shut it down, but that is only part of the story of what makes a good offense. The actual effect on your target is hard to predict, and damage assessment is difficult to carry out, meaning that it's tough to know if the attack worked or what to do next.

Nowhere was this more evident than in the United States' covert cyber campaign against Iranian nuclear facilities. Stuxnet was not something your run-of-the-mill terror group could have pulled off. It involved a Manhattan-project style of organization and expertise. The people involved ranged from intelligence agents and analysts—who teased together the exact location, make, and model of the targets in Iran—to some of the top cyber weapons designer talent in the world to engineering and nuclear physics experts, who helped the group understand the target and how best to compromise the research. The result was a weapon of sophistication and nuance not seen before that could be deployed without the initial knowledge of the Iranians.

Despite this amazing level of effort and expertise, Stuxnet ended up not just in the Iranian targets, but in thousands of computers around the world, from India to Eastern Europe. It was that unexpected result that led IT researchers to first begin to explore it and ultimately piece together what Stuxnet actually was, compromising the operation.

But it's not just that cyberoffense can be unpredictable and even counterproductive—cyberdefense is not as helpless as is often portrayed. The attackers may have the luxury of choosing the time and place of their attack, but they have to make their way through a "cyber kill chain" of multiple steps if they actually want to achieve their objectives. According to Charles Croom, a retired U.S. Air Force lieutenant general who once led the Defense Information Systems Agency, "The attacker has to take a number of steps: reconnaissance, build a weapon, deliver that weapon, pull information out of the network. Each step creates a vulnerability, and all have to be completed. But a defender can stop the attack at any step."

Moreover, defenders who are losing in the cyber realm don't have to restrict the game to just that domain or one iteration. They can try to impose other costs on the attacker, whether they be economic or diplomatic costs, traditional military action, or a cyber counterattack. Rather than just sitting there defenseless, they can take action either to deter the attack or reduce the benefits from it.

In the future, it's not difficult to imagine that cyberdefense will sometimes be able to outsmart an adversary and turn the tables on them.

The most important lesson researchers have learned in traditional offense-defense balances—and now in cybersecurity—is that the best defense actually is a good defense. Regardless of which side has the advantage, any steps that raise the capabilities of the defense make life harder on the offense and limit the incentives for attacks in the first place. In cybersecurity, these include any and all measures that tighten network security and aid in forensics to track back attackers.

The Internet evolves and so do doctrines. The smart players in the field are moving from a traditional framework of defense to an approach of resilience. Instead of building walls, they are focusing on how systems recover rapidly, or, even better, keep on functioning even after they have been compromised. The idea is to build systems where the parallel for offense and defense isn't from warfare, but biology. When it comes to bacteria and viruses in our bodies, human cells are actually outnumbered by as much as 10 to 1. But the body has built up an amazing capacity of both resistance and resilience, fighting off what is most dangerous and, as Vint Cerf, the computer scientist who is literally one of the "fathers of the Internet," puts it, figuring out how to "fight through the intrusion."

No computer network will mimic the human body perfectly, but DARPA and other groups are working on "intelligent" computer security networks that learn and adapt to resist cyberattacks. In the future, it's not difficult to imagine that cyberdefense will sometimes be able to outsmart an adversary and turn the tables on them. Other efforts aim at misdirecting attacks down false alleys of faked information or sending them into so-called honeypots to ensnare and study them. Just the mere existence of such systems, moreover, would sow doubt among adversaries that an attack is going to work.

In the end, the focus on offense and defense obscures a crucial reality of modern-day cybersecurity that distinguishes it from World War I, or, even worse, the poorly thought-out Cold War parallels that too many leaders and commentators make.

In 1914 and again in 1945, the powers of the day ended up split into two alliances, worried that one or the other side would seize the offensive advantage. But much like the users of the broader Internet itself, cyberattackers and defenders to-day range from the more than 100 militaries that have built some kind of cybermilitary unit to large and small technology firms to collectives that join Anonymous netizens interested in everything from Internet Freedom to cute cat videos. The on-line world is hardly bipolar, and nor should our thinking on it be.

So when the question is how to protect your online glass house, buying a stone sharpening kit is certainly not the only answer.

CHAPTER 4

What Should Be Done to Protect Internet Users from Cybercrime?

Overview: Public Opinion on Security and Privacy

Josh Smith

Josh Smith is a journalist for Stars and Stripes.

Proposals to increase cybersecurity by allowing businesses and government to share information may enjoy bipartisan support in Washington, but Americans aren't sold on the idea, the latest United Technologies/*National Journal* Congressional Connection Poll finds.

Concern About Privacy

Almost two-thirds of respondents—63 percent—said government and businesses should not be allowed to share information because it would hurt privacy and civil liberties. But 29 percent of those surveyed said information-sharing should be allowed to better protect computer networks.

The United Technologies/*National Journal* Congressional Connection Poll, conducted by Princeton Survey Research Associates International, surveyed 1,004 adults from July 5–8 [2012]. The poll has a margin of error of plus or minus 3.7 percentage points.

The poll's results strike at the heart of bipartisan proposals that would encourage businesses to share information by providing liability protections and revising some privacy laws. Those measures also would allow government agencies to share classified threat information with some businesses.

The specifics of the proposals differ slightly, but the White House and executive-agency officials, as well as Democrats and Republicans in Congress, are pushing for information-sharing measures.

In April [2012], the House passed the Cyber Intelligence Sharing and Protection Act, known by its acronym CISPA, defying a civil-liberties backlash and a White House veto threat.

House Speaker John Boehner, R-Ohio, had characterized his chamber's information-sharing proposals as "common-sense steps that would allow people to communicate with each other, to work together, to build the walls that are necessary in order to prevent cyberterrorism from occurring."

The survey's findings indicate lawmakers have made little headway in assuaging privacy concerns outside the Beltway.

The White House, backed by Homeland Security Secretary Janet Napolitano and the U.S. Cyber Command chief, Gen. Keith Alexander, is pushing for more real-time communication between business and government.

Information-sharing has been a relative bright spot of agreement not only among Democrats and Republicans, but with businesses. However, the survey's findings indicate lawmakers have made little headway in assuaging privacy concerns outside the Beltway. People surveyed in the latest poll sided against the White House and Senate Democrats on another key issue: whether government officials should be able to set cybersecurity standards for private businesses.

Concern About Government Standards

In the Congressional Connection Poll, 55 percent of respondents said that businesses should be allowed to set their own standards. On the other hand, 36 percent said the government should be allowed to require businesses to meet specific security standards.

Leaders of the Senate's Homeland Security, Commerce, and Intelligence committees have been pushing the Cybersecurity Act of 2012, which would allow the Homeland Security

Department to help set mandatory standards for certain critical networks, such as electric grids or water systems.

The bill is based on proposals offered by the White House, which insists: "Voluntary measures alone are insufficient responses to the growing danger of cyberthreats."

The Cybersecurity Act could come to the Senate floor this month, after having been delayed for months by Republican objections to the government standards. Its sponsors argue that the act's standards are minimal and would not apply to the vast majority of private businesses that run networks. Still, that hasn't stopped Republicans and business groups, such as the U.S. Chamber of Commerce, from complaining about regulatory overreach. "Policymakers should not complicate or duplicate existing security-related industry standards with government-specific standards and bureaucracies," the chamber and two dozen other industry groups wrote in a recent letter to Congress. "Regulations would divert businesses' focus from security to compliance."

The privacy flap is déjà vu for Homeland Security Chairman Joe Lieberman, ID-Conn., and the Cybersecurity Act's other cosponsors, who are meeting with civil-liberties groups opposing the bill. A year ago, Lieberman and his allies revised another proposal in response to critics who said it could give the president the power to shut down the Internet.

The poll's results largely mirrored the party-line rift, but Democrats and those respondents leaning Democratic were split, 46 percent in favor of government standards to 46 percent against. Fully two-thirds (67 percent) of those surveyed who identified themselves as Republicans or Republican-leaning opposed government standards. Meanwhile, 57 percent of respondents who said they are independents or members of other parties also opposed mandatory standards.

One area where Americans do back their lawmakers is concern about cyberthreats: A combined 67 percent of those surveyed said they were either very or somewhat worried about threats to the country's computer networks. Another 19 percent said they are not too worried about such threats, while 13 percent said they are not worried at all.

Broken down by education, 66 percent of those with a college degree and 71 percent who attended some college said they were worried about cyberthreats, versus 61 percent of people with a high school education or less.

By a significant margin, women were more concerned about cyberthreats: 72 percent of women said they were worried compared to 62 percent of men. Only 9 percent of women said they were not worried at all, compared to 16 percent of men.

The Cybersecurity Information Sharing Act Should Be Passed

David Inserra

David Inserra is a research associate at the Allison Center for Foreign and National Security Policy at The Heritage Foundation.

On July 8, the Senate Intelligence Committee passed the Cybersecurity Information Sharing Act (CISA) of 2014. Cybersecurity information sharing is a valuable tool to enhance the security of businesses and the U.S. government. While sharing information on cyber threats and vulnerabilities is not a silver bullet, it keeps security personnel up to date with the constantly changing cyber environment and provides critical data to enhance their efforts to keep systems secure.

As with many policies, though, the devil is in the details. CISA takes the right approach, but it could be improved through clearer privacy provisions, broader use of shared information, and more protections from regulatory use.

Information Sharing 101

Cybersecurity threats and vulnerabilities are constantly being found, exploited, and fixed—but often not before serious damage is done. When any organization finds a threat or vulnerability, sharing the technical data on that threat or vulnerability with others can help them prepare for the threat or remedy the vulnerability.

Information sharing is focused on the technical data of where an attack came from, what the target was, and how it works, not the contents of an e-mail or hard drive.

To make information sharing work, however, lawmakers should clear away ambiguity in current laws written back in the 1980s, a change that CISA and other information-sharing bills make. Other details regarding liability protections, usage of shared information, privacy provisions, and mechanisms for sharing must also be decided. CISA handles some of these details well and others less so.

Since information sharing is focused on technical data, not personal content, the broad use of this technical data to protect U.S. citizens and companies from harm entails little risk to privacy.

Liability Protections. CISA provides absolute liability protection for information sharing that follows CISA's procedures—so long as such sharing is not grossly negligent or an act of willful misconduct. Such a high bar of protection ensures that companies that share or receive information will not be sued for merely trying to improve their and other's cybersecurity. (A lower standard, such as "good faith," may sound strong, but it is much easier for a tort lawyer to insinuate a lack of good faith than it is to prove willful misconduct or gross negligence.) If sharing occurs in a way not authorized by CISA, a good-faith defense is allowed, providing at least some defense to other sharing. Overall, this robust set of liability protections would help prevent the chilling of information sharing due to the threat of potential lawsuits.

Similarly, CISA provides Freedom of Information Act protections from shared data and does not allow regulators to use information directly against sharers or receivers of threat information to regulate their "lawful activities." This construction, however, implies that regulators may directly use information against a regulated entity if they believe a law or regulation is not being followed. While law breaking should not be encouraged, companies may be afraid to share information if they fear that doing so may indicate a regulatory breach, even if it is unintentional or unknown.

Authorized Uses. CISA allows the government to use information gained by information sharing for several purposes, including:

- Enhancing cybersecurity,

- Preventing or prosecuting cases involving death or serious bodily harm,

- Combatting serious threats to minors,

- Investigating and prosecuting case of fraud and identity theft, and

- Protecting the U.S. from and taking action against those who engage in espionage and the theft of trade secrets.

This relatively broad list allows the government to use information not only for cybercrime but also for other serious crimes. Since information sharing is focused on technical data, not personal content, the broad use of this technical data to protect U.S. citizens and companies from harm entails little risk to privacy.

As a result, further expanding the authorized uses of information would enable law enforcement and security agencies to use shared information to combat additional crimes and security threats that might not fall within the authorization provided in CISA.

Privacy and Security. Given the large amount of sensitive and personal data that is stored on computer systems, citizens should be concerned when they hear about the sharing of cyber information. It is important, however, to remember that most information that is shared is technical data, not the content of e-mails or even the real identities of people who were attacked.

CISA designates the Department of Homeland Security (DHS) as the hub for sharing information with the government.

That said, when cybersecurity information is shared, some personal information might still be attached to it. While security personnel have no interest in this information, information sharing happens quickly and often automatically to ensure that constantly changing threats are countered as soon as possible.

CISA requires companies to remove all personal data before they share cybersecurity information. Removing this information is worthwhile, but it must be balanced with the need for rapid information sharing, since requiring every sharer to remove every piece of personal information would slow sharing.

CISA includes other privacy provisions that are appropriate and helpful, including:

- Time limits on retaining cyber threat information,

- Requirements that privacy and civil liberties officers and inspectors general report on how shared information is being used and how it is affecting the privacy of individuals, and

- A requirement that the government notify an entity when it shares information not related to a cyber threat.

DHS or a Public-Private Partnership. CISA designates the Department of Homeland Security (DHS) as the hub for sharing information with the government. This hub would immediately share information with other federal agencies, and in a process to be determined, information would then be shared with the private sector.

Having a central hub can help facilitate the spread of information, but while DHS is the most appropriate government agency to house this hub, there are questions regarding DHS's ability to handle this responsibility.

An alternative solution is a public-private partnership organization including a board of representatives from DHS, other government agencies, the private sector, and privacy advocates. Such an organization would have more oversight, encourage more collaboration, and, if properly structured, be more capable while not consuming more DHS resources.

Congressional Steps for Improvement

Overall, CISA is a step in the right direction, but it could be improved. Congress should consider:

- *Restricting regulatory use of shared information.* While using shared information to better understand the state of cybersecurity and cyber threats can be helpful, companies should not fear that any information they share could result in regulatory action.

- *Broadening authorized uses of shared information.* CISA includes relatively broad areas where the government can use shared information, but broader non-regulatory use would be better at enhancing security. A better policy would be to allow government agencies to use and share information so long as one significant use is for a cybersecurity purpose.

- *Streamlining privacy provisions.* Privacy provisions that overly impede information sharing should be revised. Instead of requiring all information be scrubbed of all personal data, a more appropriate standard is to require the reasonable removal of personal information in a way that does not slow sharing.

CISA seeks to improve cybersecurity through information sharing and takes several steps in the right direction. Strong liability protections and relatively broad authorized uses could be improved by streamlining burdensome privacy provisions, strengthening protection from overbearing regulation, broadening authorized uses, and identifying a better mechanism for sharing.

The Cybersecurity Information Sharing Act Should Not Be Passed

John W. Whitehead

John W. Whitehead is an attorney, president of the Rutherford Institute, and author of A Government of Wolves: The Emerging American Police State.

Nothing you write, say, text, tweet or share via phone or computer is private anymore. As constitutional law professor Garrett Epps points out, "Big Brother is watching. . . . Big Brother may be watching you right now, and you may never know. Since 9/11, our national life has changed forever. Surveillance is the new normal."

This is the reality of the Internet-dependent, plugged-in life of most Americans today.

The Expansion of Surveillance

A process which started shortly after 9/11 with programs such as Total Information Awareness (the predecessor to the government's present surveillance programs) has grown into a full-fledged campaign of warrantless surveillance, electronic tracking and data mining, thanks to federal agents who have been given *carte blanche* access to the vast majority of electronic communications in America. Their methods completely undermine constitution safeguards, and yet no federal agency, president, court or legislature has stepped up to halt this assault on our rights.

For the most part, surveillance, data mining, etc., is a technological, jargon-laden swamp through which the average

American would prefer not to wander. Consequently, most Americans remain relatively oblivious to the government's ever-expanding surveillance powers, appear unconcerned about the fact that the government is spying on them, and seem untroubled that there is no way of opting out of this system. This state of delirium lasts only until those same individuals find themselves arrested or detained for something they did, said or bought that runs afoul of the government's lowering threshold for what constitutes criminal activity.

Be warned: this cybersecurity bill is little more than a wolf in sheep's clothing.

All the while, Congress, the courts, and the president (starting with George W. Bush and expanding exponentially under Barack Obama) continue to erect an electronic concentration camp the likes of which have never been seen before.

A Dangerous Cybersecurity Bill

A good case in point is the Cybersecurity Information Sharing Act (CISA), formerly known as CISPA (Cyber Intelligence Sharing and Protection Act). Sold to the public as necessary for protecting us against cyberattacks or Internet threats such as hacking, this Orwellian exercise in tyranny-masquerading-as-security actually makes it easier for the government to spy on Americans, while officially turning Big Business into a government snitch.

Be warned: this cybersecurity bill is little more than a wolf in sheep's clothing or, as longtime critic Senator Ron Wyden labeled it, "a surveillance bill by another name."

Lacking any significant privacy protections, CISA, which sacrifices privacy without improving security, will do for surveillance what the Patriot Act did for the government's police powers: it will expand, authorize and normalize the government's intrusions into the most intimate aspects of our lives to such an extent that there will be no turning back. In other words, it will ensure that the Fourth Amendment, which protects us against unfounded, warrantless government surveillance, does not apply to the Internet or digital/electronic communications of any kind.

In a nutshell, CISA would make it legal for the government to spy on the citizenry without their knowledge and without a warrant under the guise of fighting cyberterrorism. It would also protect private companies from being sued for sharing your information with the government, namely the National Security Agency (NSA) and the Department of Homeland Security (DHS), in order to prevent "terrorism" or an "imminent threat of death or serious bodily harm."

Law enforcement agencies would also be given broad authority to sift through one's data for any possible crimes. What this means is that you don't even have to be suspected of a crime to be under surveillance. The bar is set so low as to allow government officials to embark on a fishing expedition into your personal affairs—emails, phone calls, text messages, purchases, banking transactions, etc.—based only on their need to find and fight "crime."

While Obama calls for vague protections for privacy and civil liberties without providing any specific recommendations, he appoints the DHS to oversee the information sharing.

Take this anything-goes attitude towards government surveillance, combine it with Big Business' complicity over the government's blatantly illegal acts, the ongoing trend towards overcriminalization, in which minor acts are treated as major crimes, and the rise of private prisons, which have created a profit motive for jailing Americans, and you have all the makings of a fascist police state.

No Protection from Government

So who can we count on to protect us from the threat of government surveillance?

It won't be the courts. Not in an age of secret courts, secret court rulings, and an overall deference by the courts to anything the government claims is necessary to its fight against terrorism. Most recently, the U.S. Supreme Court refused to hear a case challenging the government's massive electronic wiretapping program. As Court reporter Lyle Denniston notes:

> *Daoud v. United States* was the first case, in the nearly four-decade history of electronic spying by the U.S. government to gather foreign intelligence, in which a federal judge had ordered the government to turn over secret papers about how it had obtained evidence through wiretaps of telephones and Internet links. That order, however, was overturned by the U.S. Court of Appeals for the Seventh Circuit, whose ruling was the one the Justices on Monday declined to review. . . . One of the unusual features of the government's global electronic spying program is that the individuals whose conversations or e-mails have been monitored almost never hear about it, because the program is so shrouded in secrecy—except when the news media manages to find out some details. But, if the government plans to use evidence it gathered under that program against a defendant in a criminal trial, it must notify the defendant that he or she has been monitored.

It won't be Congress, either (CISA is their handiwork, remember), which has failed to do anything to protect the citizenry from an overbearing police state, all the while enabling the government to continue its power grabs. It was Congress that started us down this whole Big Brother road with its passage and subsequent renewals of the USA Patriot Act, which drove a stake through the heart of the Bill of Rights. The Patriot Act rendered First Amendment activists potential terrorists; justified broader domestic surveillance; authorized black bag "sneak-and-peak" searches of homes and offices by government agents; granted the FBI the right to come to your place of employment, demand your personal records and question your supervisors and fellow employees, all without notifying you; allowed the government access to your medical records, school records and practically every personal record about you; allowed the government to secretly demand to see records of books or magazines you've checked out in any public library and Internet sites you've visited.

The Patriot Act also gave the government the green light to monitor religious and political institutions with no suspicion of criminal wrongdoing; prosecute librarians or keepers of any other records if they told anyone that the government had subpoenaed information related to a terror investigation; monitor conversations between attorneys and clients; search and seize Americans' papers and effects without showing probable cause; and jail Americans indefinitely without a trial, among other things.

And it certainly won't be the president. Indeed, President Obama recently issued an executive order calling on private companies (phone companies, banks, Internet providers, you name it) to share their customer data (*your* personal data) with each other and, most importantly, the government. Here's the problem, however: while Obama calls for vague protections for privacy and civil liberties without providing any specific recommendations, he appoints the DHS to oversee the information sharing and develop guidelines with the attorney general for how the government will collect and share the data.

Talk about putting the wolf in charge of the hen house.

Mind you, this is the same agency, rightly dubbed a "wasteful, growing, fear-mongering beast," that is responsible for militarizing the police, weaponizing SWAT teams, spying on activists, stockpiling ammunition, distributing license plate readers to state police, carrying out military drills in American cities, establishing widespread surveillance networks through the use of fusion centers, funding city-wide surveillance systems, accelerating the domestic use of drones, and generally establishing itself as the nation's standing army, i.e., a national police force.

Three Camps of Thought

This brings me back to the knotty problem of how to protect Americans from cyberattacks without further eroding our privacy rights.

The U.S. government has more data on American citizens than the Stasi secret police had on East Germans.

Dependent as we are on computer technology for almost all aspects of our lives, it's feasible that a cyberattack on American computer networks really *could* cripple both the nation's infrastructure and its economy. So do we allow the government liberal powers to control and spy on all electronic communications flowing through the United States? Can we trust the government not to abuse its privileges and respect our privacy rights? Does it even matter, given that we have no real say in the matter?

As I point out in my book *A Government of Wolves: The Emerging American Police State*, essentially, there are three camps of thought on the question of how much power the government should have, and which camp you fall into says a lot about your view of government—or, at least, your view of whichever administration happens to be in power at the time, for the time being, the one calling the shots being the Obama administration.

In the first camp are those who trust the government to do the right thing—or, at least, they trust the Obama administration to look out for their best interests. To this group, CISA is simply a desperately needed blueprint for safeguarding us against a possible cyberattack, with a partnership between the government and Big Business serving as the most logical means of thwarting such an attack. Any suggestion that the government and its corporate cohorts might abuse this power is dismissed as conspiratorial hysterics. The problem, as technology reporter Adam Clark Estes points out, is that CISA is a "privacy nightmare" that "stomps all over civil liberties" without making "the country any safer against cyberattacks."

Surveillance has become the new normal, and the effects of this endless surveillance are taking a toll, resulting in a more anxious and submissive citizenry.

In the second camp are those who not only don't trust the government but think the government is out to get them. Sadly, they've got good reason to distrust the government, especially when it comes to abusing its powers and violating our rights. For example, consider that government surveillance of innocent Americans has exploded over the past decade. In fact, *Wall Street Journal* reporter Julia Angwin has concluded that, as a result of its spying and data collection, the U.S. government has more data on American citizens than the Stasi secret police had on East Germans. To those in this second group, CISA is nothing less than the writing on the wall that surveillance is here to stay, meaning that the government will continue to monitor, regulate and control all means of communications.

Then there's the third camp, which neither sees government as an angel or a devil, but merely as an entity that needs to be controlled, or as Thomas Jefferson phrased it, bound "down from mischief with the chains of the Constitution." A distrust of all who hold governmental power was rife among those who drafted the Constitution and the Bill of Rights. James Madison, the nation's fourth president and the author of the Bill of Rights, was particularly vocal in warning against government. He once observed, "All men having power ought to be distrusted to a certain degree."

To those in the third camp, the only way to ensure balance in government is by holding government officials accountable to abiding by the rule of law. Unfortunately, with all branches of the government, including the courts, stridently working to maintain its acquired powers, and the private sector marching in lockstep, there seems to be little to protect the American people from the fast-growing electronic surveillance state.

In the meantime, surveillance has become the new normal, and the effects of this endless surveillance are taking a toll, resulting in a more anxious and submissive citizenry. As Fourth Amendment activist Alex Marthews points out,

> Mass surveillance is becoming a punchline. Making it humorous makes mass surveillance seem easy and friendly and a normal part of life ... we make uneasy jokes about how we should watch what we say, about the government looking over our shoulders, about cameras and informers and eyes in the sky. Even though we may not in practice think that these agencies pay us any mind, mass surveillance still creates a chilling effect: We limit what we search for online and inhibit expression of controversial viewpoints. This more submissive mentality isn't a side effect. As far as anyone is able to measure, it's the main effect of mass surveillance. The effect of such programs is not primarily to thwart attacks by foreign terrorists on U.S. soil; it's to discourage challenges to the security services' authority over our lives here at home.

Websites Should Not Be Blocked to Protect Copyright

Erik Stallman

Erik Stallman is general counsel and director of the Open Internet Project at the Center for Democracy & Technology.

Based on information obtained through the deplorable hack of Sony Pictures Entertainment, some of the major content companies may be trying to revive a particularly bad idea: that copyright infringement can and should be combated by ordering Internet service providers (ISPs) to block access to entire websites.

The Stop Online Piracy Act

The Stop Online Piracy Act (SOPA), which was overwhelmingly rejected by the Internet community in 2012, had exactly this concept at its core. Website blocking presents an unwarranted and unjustifiable threat to basic Internet security and freedom of expression. When Internet users, technical experts, companies, academics, and others stood together to oppose SOPA, we sent the clear message that censorship and poorly devised technological mandates have no place in a responsible copyright enforcement regime.

As a reminder: SOPA would have allowed law enforcement to seek orders against ISPs, requiring them to take "measures designed to prevent the domain name of a foreign infringing site (or portion thereof) from resolving to that domain name's Internet Protocol address." That is, when a user typed into her browser the name of a foreign-hosted website alleged to be "dedicated to infringing activity," the ISP would be required to return a result other than the site's actual IP address—sending the user an inaccurate result. This is a terrible idea.

The Motion Picture Association of America (MPAA) apparently is still pursuing website-blocking to combat piracy.

It's a terrible idea because it would alter how information is retrieved on the Web and threaten the security of the Domain Name System (DNS). DNS is the basic "phone book of the Internet," linking the names of websites with their unique IP addresses. The accuracy of the DNS address book is what ensures that typing "bankofamerica.com" into your browser takes you to the website of your bank rather than the website of a sophisticated phishing operation. When DNS filtering appeared in SOPA, renowned cybersecurity experts, Sandia National Laboratories, Vint Cerf, a group of 83 Internet inventors and engineers, and eventually the White House expressed serious concerns.

Thankfully, those concerns won out and SOPA went down in spectacular fashion. But it remained alarming to many who followed the debate that it took so long for legislators and stakeholders to appreciate security concerns embedded in DNS filtering. As Representative Jason Chaffetz memorably said at the time, "we're going to do surgery on the Internet, and we haven't had a doctor in the room tell us how we're going to change these organs. We're basically going to reconfigure the Internet and how it's going to work, without bringing in the nerds."

A New Attempt at DNS Filtering

Three years later, the Motion Picture Association of America (MPAA) apparently is still pursuing website-blocking to combat piracy. And the MPAA seems only mildly more interested in the security implications of DNS filtering than it was in 2011. According to a January 2014 MPAA memo, "[v]ery little systematic work has been completed to understand the technical issues related to site blocking in the US. . . . We will identify and retain a consulting technical expert to work with us to study these issues."

Assuming the memo's accuracy, this nonchalance toward security implications may be the most alarming feature of the MPAA's attempt to reboot SOPA's site-blocking regime through other legal theories and forums. Notwithstanding leading security experts and the White House having stated in no uncertain terms that court-mandated DNS filtering by ISPs threatened Internet security, the MPAA's campaign to put that technological mandate in place continued unabated.

The studios' interest in streamlined procedures for removing infringing content from the Internet is understandable. But existing procedures for removing infringing content under the Digital Millennium Copyright Act (DMCA) are there for good reasons, including due process and protecting legitimate innovation on the Internet. Yesterday, the U.S. Patent & Trademark Office convened its sixth multi-stakeholder forum on improving the operation of the DMCA's notice-and-takedown system. Improving notice-and-takedown is a far preferable approach to addressing ongoing infringement concerns than pursuing technological mandates that have already been decisively rejected.

That the MPAA's renewed or continued interest in site blocking was disclosed through a malicious hack of a private enterprise's network is regrettable. Any person or entity commenting on that information must struggle with its provenance. However, part of preventing hacks like this from occurring in the future is prioritizing security in policy discussions that impact the Internet. This was one of the core lessons of the SOPA debate—we should learn from it, and move on.

Copyright Must Be Protected on the Internet

David Newhoff

David Newhoff is a writer, filmmaker, and blogger at The Illusion of More: Dissecting the Digital Utopia.

Jenna Wortham, technology writer for *The New York Times*, offers [an] article in which she questions the illegality of IP theft online. Titled, *The Unrepentant Bootlegger*, Wortham begins with a description of what some may consider an unjustifiably heavy-handed raid by DHS [US Department of Homeland Security] officers in the arrest of Hana Beshara, a cofounder of the illegal media site NinjaVideo, shut down in 2009. One can argue that non-violent criminals should be arrested in a less dramatic way (though I wonder how that sentiment might apply to insider-trading felons), but that isn't the point of Wortham's article. No, her thesis asks wether or not Beshara's actions ought to be illegal in the first place; and I'd like to jump to her quote about SOPA [Stop Online Piracy Act] near the end of the article because so much of her inquiry poses naive questions based on false premises like the following:

> After the seizure of NinjaVideo and the other sites, the M.P.A.A. [Motion Picture Association of America] pushed federal legislation to continue to crack down on illegal downloading. But the bill, SOPA, was so loosely worded that it could have required all websites to be responsible for monitoring their services for potential violations—an expensive and nearly impossible challenge—prompting sites like Wikipedia, Tumblr and Craigslist to rally online senti-

ment against the legislation. Outrage about the bill came to a head in 2012, and lawmakers backed off.

The Truth About SOPA

This narrative about SOPA has been repeated so many times that even a writer for the *NY Times* can get away with presenting it as fact. But it just ain't so. There was nothing about the wording of the SOPA/PIPA bills that could be used to hold US-based websites any more responsible for infringement than they already were in 2011, or than they still are at this moment. In fact, language in the bills explicitly stated that they do not trump precedent, domestic law. The bills were specifically designed to starve foreign-based sites, dedicated to piracy, of their revenue streams strictly because the site owners themselves operate beyond the reach of U.S. law enforcement. Wortham's own emotional introduction to her article, describing the flack-jacketed arrest of Hana Beshara ought to indicate to anyone how utterly unnecessary it would be to have introduced SOPA/PIPA as domestic-focused laws. Clearly, what Beshara and her NinjaVideo colleagues were doing is already enforceably illegal in the U.S., hence the guys busting into her condo and the 16 months she spent in prison.

It simply isn't possible to produce all major motion pictures and television in a manner that makes all of these works instantaneously available in every market worldwide and for prices that compete with the unlicensed option of free.

The notion that SOPA could have shut down Facebook, et al was the result of well-orchestrated, and well-funded fearmongering; and I stand by the assertion that (issues of piracy aside) the anti-SOPA campaign was the most successful corporate-serving bamboozlement of the electorate in my lifetime. The campaign was holistically corrupt in that the very tools being employed to manipulate the political process simultaneously created the illusion that people believed themselves empowered through information to take action. Never have I seen so many intelligent friends motivated to reaction based on such illogical, let alone unsubstantiated, claims. Did it not occur to any of my progressive, educated colleagues at the time that in all likelihood no member of Congress, no matter what we may think of his/her other politics, would sign the "shut down Facebook and Twitter" bill? Yet, here we are, almost four years later, and *NY Times* writers are behaving as though the Internet industry talking points are historical facts. And that brings us to the crux of Wortham's article, summed up in this quote:

> Ms. Beshara, however, still can't accept that what she was doing deserved the heavy hammer of the law. She served 16 months in prison for conspiracy and criminal copyright infringement, but she still talks about NinjaVideo as something grand.

Something grand indeed. It is astonishing that even when independent artists recite their stories of working for years on a project only to have it hijacked by a pirate site, they're accused of whining; but when profiteering site founders are busted, they're treated like martyrs to the cause of culture and smarter business practices. This narrative that we should credit the NinjaVideos and Megauploads of the world for giving us iTunes and Netflix is another false premise; and it is always perplexing to read declarations about the public "wanting 24/7 on-demand everything for free or really cheap" as though those making such statements believe they're revealing some profound ethnographic discovery. Really? People would like instant gratification and would prefer to pay next to nothing for it. That *is* a shocker. If only there were a Pulitzer Prize for the Numbingly Obvious.

The Normalization of Piracy

The problem is that when writers like Wortham, under the imprimatur of venerable publications, repeat this self-evident observation about consumers and then pose the rhetorical question about the illegality of piracy, they fail to recognize through the fog of their own presumed humanism that they're in fact promoting an anti-fair-trade market. This is because it simply isn't possible to produce all major motion pictures and television in a manner that makes all of these works instantaneously available in every market worldwide and for prices that compete with the unlicensed option of free. To make such a demand on motion picture producers, both great and small, implies that the stake-holding subcontractors whose skills, labors, and constituent products used to produce these films must have their interests (i.e. means of living) subverted to the exigencies of black-market economics.

Going forward, I expect we will see more and more film projects organized at the contractual stage of development to facilitate early release on legal, web-based platforms—we're already seeing this occur in some cases—but the conclusion Wortham implies is that the attitudes about piracy are so socially ingrained at this point that we ought to simply accept them and perhaps even praise them as enlightened. This isn't surprising of course. Normalizing negative behaviors or trends does have a tendency to screw up perceptions about the consequences of those behaviors. Articles like Wortham's remind me of a moment back in college when I bumped into a fellow film major—he wasn't the sharpest tool in the shed—one afternoon and he told me he was bummed because his friend had been expelled. I asked why, and he said that the friend had "set his dorm room door on fire."

"Um, Dude, that's arson," was all I could think to say.

"Yeah," he replies, "but there's so much other shit he did that the school never caught him for."

This was sound reasoning in his mind. His friend's miscreant, even dangerous, behaviors had become so normalized that it seemed entirely unreasonable for the college to take disciplinary action. And that's the thing about the many thousands of words at this point that have been dedicated to recontextualizing media piracy. Call it what you want, but, at a certain point, all we can conclude is, "Dude, that's larceny."

SOPA: A Bad Solution to a Very Real Problem

Jeffrey Rosen

Jeffrey Rosen is legal affairs editor at The New Republic *and president and chief executive officer of the National Constitution Center.*

The Web protests that led to a collapse of support in the House and Senate for two ill-designed antipiracy bills are a cause for celebration. In their current forms, both the Stop Online Piracy Act (SOPA) in the House and the Protect IP Act (PIPA) in the Senate are heavy-handed and indefensible, attempts to shut down a handful of rogue pirate sites by changing the open structure of the Internet. In allowing the Justice Department to force Internet service providers to block access to websites that "enable" pirated content, the proposed legislation would pose serious threats to free speech.

But even as we celebrate the declining congressional support for these bills, we shouldn't forget that this isn't simply a fight about the future of free speech; it's also a battle about whether the financial interests of the new media will triumph over those of the old media. And, if they do, it's not clear that the public interest will always be served. As the protest song that sprang up this week put it, "Our web means more than lawyers, lobbies, and lies, so speak up before the Internet dies." There are lawyers and lobbies on both sides of the debate, however, and neither side is devoted to the promotion of creativity for its own sake.

Ultimately, it's too simplistic to see the copyright wars as a battle between idealistic tech companies that want information to be free, and the greedy old media that wants to preserve a dying business model. Instead, as Robert Levine argues in his new book *Free Ride: How Digital Parasites Are Destroying the Culture Business, and How the Culture Business Can Fight Back*, the real battle is between two competing business models. On the one hand, there are the publishers, record companies, and movie companies that fund the content people want to watch and read. On the other, there are the tech companies, like Google and Facebook, that want to distribute content created with other people's money and sell more ads as a result. By destroying the business model that makes it possible for AMC to invest in excellent shows like "Mad Men," Levine argues, the tech companies will create a digital wasteland dominated by self-produced cat videos.

It's not obvious that online piracy is the major factor in allowing tech companies to distribute content for less than they pay for it.

There's much to be said for Levine's analysis of the competing financial interests on both sides of the debate: The current system looks much better for the tech companies that distribute other people's content than for the old media companies that fund it. And to the degree that it's harder for artists and journalists to get paid for their work, the public may not benefit in the long run. What's still unclear—and is important to figure out—is how great a role Internet piracy is playing in destroying the business model that used to allow old media companies to invest in authors, musicians, and movie producers, and support them over the course of a career.

Levine argues that "as piracy lowers the value of media, technology companies have essentially managed to set the price of music and videos and tried to do the same for books." In a version of Wal-Mart capitalism, the argument goes, no matter what a movie or book costs to produce, Amazon and iTunes can sell it for as little as possible and make their money elsewhere—by selling iPods or kindles, for example.

But it's not obvious that online piracy is the major factor in allowing tech companies to distribute content for less than they pay for it. Levine cites the example of the music industry, which was so spooked by the proliferation of pirated music on Napster that it struck a poor deal with Apple, replacing the sale of $15 albums with 99-cent songs. Yet there's little evidence that the same result would not have occurred in a world without Napster: Individual bands might have struck enough deals with Apple that the music industry would still have been forced to sell its content below the cost of production.

What we need, therefore, is more empirical research about the relationship between copyright enforcement and digital creativity. There is certainly a price below which authors and journalists won't produce good work in the first place, and also a price below which the failure to promote authors, movies, and journalists ensures they never find the audience they deserve. But whether more vigorous copyright enforcement would solve these problems needs more study.

In the meantime, there are plenty of moderate alternatives to the unlamented SOPA and PIPA. The best solution, one that protects copyright without changing the architecture of the Internet, might lie in simple law enforcement, of the kind that ensures there's less commercial child pornography available online than there was fifteen years ago. This is the approach taken in a 2010 report by Victoria Espinel, the White House's copyright czar, which suggests that the best way of combating international piracy is to "enhance foreign law enforcement cooperation" and "strengthen intellectual property enforcement through international organizations." Since the number of commercial pirate sites operating overseas is small—a couple dozen, by some estimates—tracking and identifying them, and prosecuting them in cooperation with overseas police forces, is a far more focused solution to the problem of Internet piracy than shutting down free speech for everyone. But will this be enough to save the old media's business model, and the artists, musicians, and writers it has long supported? That remains an open question.

Incentives Must Be Created to Reduce Internet Piracy

Peter Singer

Peter Singer is the Ira W. DeCamp Professor of Bioethics at Princeton University.

L ast year [2011], I told a colleague that I would include Internet ethics in a course that I was teaching. She suggested that I read a recently published anthology on computer ethics—and attached the entire volume to the email.

Should I have refused to read a pirated book? Was I receiving stolen goods, as advocates of stricter laws against Internet piracy claim?

Questions About Digital Theft

If I steal someone's book the old-fashioned way, I have the book, and the original owner no longer does. I am better off, but she is worse off. When people use pirated books, the publisher and the author often are worse off—they lose earnings from selling the book.

But, if my colleague had not sent me the book, I would have borrowed the copy in my university's library. I saved myself the time needed to do that, and it seems that no one was worse off. (Curiously, given the book's subject matter, it is not for sale in digital form). In fact, others benefited from my choice as well: the book remained on the library shelf, available to other users.

On the other hand, if the book had not been on the shelf and those other users had asked library staff to recall or reserve it, the library might have noted the demand for the book and ordered a second copy. But there is only a small probability that my use of the book would have persuaded the library to buy another copy. And, in any case, we are now a long way from the standard cases of stealing.

I asked the 300 students in my ethics class which of them had *not* downloaded something from the Internet, knowing or suspecting that they were violating copyright. Only five or six hands went up. Many of the rest thought that what they had done was wrong, but said that "everyone does it." Others said that they would not have bought the music or book anyway, so they were not harming anyone. It did not seem that any of them were prepared to stop.

The Case for Copyright Laws

The case for enforcing copyright laws was strengthened by the details that emerged following the arrest in New Zealand last month [January 2012] of Kim Dotcom (born Kim Schmitz), founder of the Web site Megaupload (now closed down by the FBI). Megaupload allowed its 180 million registered users to upload and download movies, television shows, and music, and some of the money earned by Dotcom (from advertising and subscriptions) was on display at his mansion near Auckland, where he kept his Rolls-Royce and other exotic cars.

> *We need to find a way to maximize the truly amazing potential of the Internet, while properly rewarding creators.*

Dotcom's lawyer claims that Megaupload was merely providing storage for its subscribers' files, and had no control over what they were storing. But Megaupload offered cash rewards to users who uploaded files that proved popular with other users.

Last month, the United States considered legislation that aimed at stopping Internet piracy. The bills had been written at the urging of Hollywood studios and the publishing and recording industries, which claim that violations of copyright on the Internet cost the US 100,000 jobs. Opponents said the proposed law would reach far beyond sites like Megaupload, making Google and YouTube liable for copyright infringement—and allowing the government to block (without court authorization) access to Web sites that it deemed to be facilitating copyright infringement.

The Need to Reward Creators

For the moment, Internet activists, together with Google, Facebook, and other major online players, have carried the day, persuading the US Congress to shelve its anti-piracy legislation. But the fight will continue: last month, the European Union and 22 member states signed the Anti-Counterfeiting Trade Agreement, which establishes international standards and a new organization to enforce intellectual-property rights. The agreement has already been signed by Australia, Canada, Japan, Morocco, New Zealand, Singapore, and the US. Now it must be ratified by, among others, the European Parliament.

I am an author, as well as a reader. One marvel of the Internet is that some of my older works, long out of print, are now far more widely available than they ever were before—in pirated versions. Of course, I am more fortunate than many authors or creative artists, because my academic salary means that I am not forced to rely on royalties to feed my family. Nevertheless, it isn't hard to find better purposes for my royalty earnings than Kim Dotcom's environmentally damaging lifestyle. We need to find a way to maximize the truly amazing potential of the Internet, while properly rewarding creators.

Australia, Canada, Israel, New Zealand, and many European countries now have a public lending right, designed to compensate authors and publishers for the loss of sales caused by the presence of their books in public libraries. We need something similar for the Internet. A user fee could pay for it, and, if the fee were low enough, the incentive to use pirated copies would diminish. Couple that with law enforcement against the mega-abusing Web sites, and the problem might be soluble. Otherwise, most creative people will need to earn a living doing something else, and we will all be the losers.

Organizations to Contact

The editors have compiled the following list of organizations concerned with the issues debated in this book. The descriptions are derived from materials provided by the organizations. All have publications or information available for interested readers. The list was compiled on the date of publication of the present volume; the information provided here may change. Be aware that many organizations take several weeks or longer to respond to inquiries, so allow as much time as possible.

Berkman Center for Internet & Society
Harvard University, 23 Everett St., 2nd Floor
Cambridge, MA   02138
(617) 495-7547 • fax: (617) 495-7641
e-mail: cyber@law.harvard.edu
website: https://cyber.law.harvard.edu

The Berkman Center for Internet & Society at Harvard University conducts research on cyberspace, studies its developments, and assesses the need for laws and sanctions. Its Cybersecurity Project aims to explore Internet policy and cybersecurity. The Center publishes a weekly newsletter and a variety of articles, including "Privacy and Children's Data."

Brookings Institution
1775 Massachusetts Ave. NW, Washington, DC   20036
(202) 797-6000
e-mail: communications@brookings.edu
website: www.brookings.edu

The Brookings Institution is a nonprofit public policy organization that conducts independent research. The Brookings Institution uses its research to provide recommendations that advance the goals of strengthening American democracy, fostering social welfare and security, and securing a cooperative international system. The organization publishes a variety of books, reports, and commentaries, some of which deal with the issue of cybercrime and security.

Cato Institute

1000 Massachusetts Ave. NW, Washington, DC   20001-5403
(202) 842-0200 • fax: (202) 842-3490
website: www.cato.org

The Cato Institute is a public policy research organization dedicated to the principles of individual liberty, limited government, free markets, and peace. The Cato Institute aims to provide clear, thoughtful, and independent analysis on vital public policy issues. Cato publishes numerous policy studies, two quarterly journals—*Regulation* and *Cato Journal*—and the bimonthly *Cato Policy Report*.

Center for Democracy and Technology (CDT)

1634 I St. NW, #1100, Washington, DC   20006
(202) 637-9800 • fax: (202) 637-0968
website: www.cdt.org

The Center for Democracy and Technology (CDT) is a nonprofit organization that supports a user-controlled Internet and freedom of expression. CDT supports laws, corporate policies, and technology tools that protect the privacy of Internet users and advocates for stronger legal controls on government surveillance. At its website, the CDT provides numerous articles on topics such as digital copyright, security and surveillance, consumer privacy, free expression, and Internet architecture.

Center for Security Policy

1901 Pennsylvania Ave. NW, Suite 201
Washington, DC   20006
(202) 835-9077
e-mail: info@centerforsecuritypolicy.org
website: www.centerforsecuritypolicy.org

The Center for Security Policy is a nonprofit, nonpartisan, national security organization that works to establish successful national security policies through the use of diplomatic, informational, military, and economic strength. The Center for Security Policy believes that America's national power must be preserved and properly used because it holds a unique global role in maintaining peace and stability. The Center publishes periodic *Occasional Papers* and articles, all of which are available at its website.

Center for Strategic and International Studies (CSIS)

1616 Rhode Island Ave. NW, Washington, DC   20036
(202) 887-0200 • fax (202) 775-3199
website: www.csis.org

The Center for Strategic and International Studies (CSIS) is a nonprofit organization that provides strategic insights and bipartisan policy solutions to decision makers. CSIS conducts research and analysis for decision makers in government, international institutions, the private sector, and civil society on a variety of topics, including cybersecurity. CSIS publishes reports, books, commentary, and *The Washington Quarterly*.

Computer Crime and Intellectual Property Section (CCIPS)

US Department of Justice, 950 Pennsylvania Ave. NW
Washington, DC   20530-0001
(202) 514-2000
e-mail: AskDOJ@usdoj.gov
website: www.justice.gov/criminal/cybercrime

The Computer Crime and Intellectual Property Section (CCIPS) of the US Department of Justice is responsible for implementing national strategies to combat computer and intellectual property crimes worldwide. CCIPS prevents, investigates, and prosecutes computer crimes by working with other government agencies, the private sector, academic institutions, and foreign counterparts. CCIPS publishes annual reports and manuals on prosecuting cybercrime.

Electronic Frontier Foundation (EFF)

454 Shotwell St., San Francisco, CA 94110-1914
(415) 436-9333 • fax: (415) 436-9993
e-mail: info@eff.org
website: www.eff.org

The Electronic Frontier Foundation (EFF) works to promote the public interest in critical battles affecting digital rights. EFF provides legal assistance in cases where it believes it can help shape the law. EFF publishes a newsletter and reports, including "Congress Should Say No to 'Cybersecurity' Information Sharing Bills."

Federal Bureau of Investigation (FBI)

935 Pennsylvania Ave. NW, Washington, DC 20535-0001
(202) 324-3000
website: www.fbi.gov

The Federal Bureau of Investigation (FBI) is the nation's law enforcement agency. One of its areas of investigation is cyber-crime. The FBI's Cyber Crime unit investigates high-tech crimes, including cyber-based terrorism, espionage, computer intrusions, and major cyber fraud. The website of the Cyber Crime unit includes analysis of its priorities, explanations of the latest cyber threats and scams, recent cases and prosecutions, and strategies to help citizens protect themselves and report incidents.

WiredSafety

96 Linwood Plaza, #417, Ft. Lee, NJ 07024-3701
(201) 463-8663
e-mail: askparry@wiredsafety.org
website: www.wiredsafety.org

WiredSafety is an online safety, education, and help group run by volunteers. WiredSafety provides one-to-one help, extensive information, and education to cyberspace users of all ages on a variety of Internet and interactive technology safety, privacy, and security issues. WiredSafety has a variety of publications and tools available at its website for young people, parents, the media, and schools.

Bibliography

Books

Susan W. Brenner — *Cybercrime: Criminal Threats from Cyberspace.* Westport, CT: Praeger, 2010.

Jeffrey Carr — *Inside Cyber Warfare.* Sebastopol, CA: O'Reilly, 2012.

Julia Davidson and Petter Gottschalk, eds. — *Internet Child Abuse: Current Research and Policy.* New York: Routledge, 2011.

Martin Gitlin and Margaret J. Goldstein — *Cyber Attack.* Minneapolis, MN: Twenty-First Century Books, 2015.

Marc Goodman — *Future Crimes: Everything Is Connected, Everyone Is Vulnerable and What We Can Do About It.* New York: Doubleday, 2015.

Shane Harris — *@War: The Rise of the Military-Internet Complex.* Boston: Houghton Mifflin Harcourt, 2014.

Greg Lastowka — *Virtual Justice: The New Laws of Online Worlds.* New Haven, CT: Yale University Press, 2010.

Steven Levy — *Hackers: Heroes of the Computer Revolution.* Sebastopol, CA: O'Reilly, 2010.

Joseph Menn   *Fatal System Error: The Hunt for the New Crime Lords Who Are Bringing Down the Internet*. New York: PublicAffairs, 2010.

T.F. Peterson   *Nightwork: A History of Hacks and Pranks at MIT*. Cambridge, MA: MIT Press, 2011.

Kevin Poulsen   *Kingpin: How One Hacker Took Over the Billion-Dollar Cybercrime Underground*. New York: Crown, 2011.

Thomas Rid   *Cyber War Will Not Take Place*. London: Hurst, 2013.

Johann Rost and   *The Dark Side of Software Robert L. Glass   Engineering: Evil on Computing Projects*. Hoboken, NJ: Wiley, 2011.

Peter W. Singer   *Cybersecurity and Cyberwar: What and Allan   Everyone Needs to Know*. New York: Friedman   Oxford University Press, 2013.

Nancy Willard   *Cyber Savvy: Embracing Digital Safety and Civility*. Thousand Oaks, CA: Corwin Press: 2011.

Periodicals and Internet Sources

Russell Berman   "The US Government Is Under (Cyber) Attack," *Atlantic*, November 17, 2014.

James Jay   "The Sony Hack, Edward Snowden Carafano   and Ordered Liberty," *National Interest*, December 24, 2014. www.nationalinterest.org.

Soraya Chemaly — "There's No Comparing Male and Female Harassment Online," *Time*, September 9, 2014.

Michael Crowley and Josh Gerstein — "No Rules of Cyber War," *Politico*, December 23, 2014. www.politico.com.

Chris Dodd — "Consumers Need to Understand That Piracy Hurts Middle-Income Families," *Variety*, January 28, 2015.

Steven Durbin — "Cybercrime: The Next Entrepreneurial Growth Business?," *Wired*, October 2014.

Economist — "Think of a Number and Double It," January 17, 2015.

Roland Flamini — "Improving Cybersecurity," *CQ Researcher*, February 15, 2013.

Frank Gaffney Jr. — "We Are on Notice: Terrorists Target Grids," Center for Security Policy, January 27, 2015. www.centerforsecuritypolicy.org.

Tom Gjelten — "First Strike: US Cyber Warriors Seize the Offensive," *World Affairs*, January/February 2013.

Misha Glenny — "The Cyber Arms Race Has Begun," *Nation*, October 31, 2011.

Michael Joseph Gross — "Enter the Cyber-Dragon," *Vanity Fair*, September 2011.

Amanda Hess
"Why Women Aren't Welcome on the Internet," *Pacific Standard*, January 6, 2014.

Jarno Limnéll
"A Dangerous New Era: US Must Take Lead in Cybersecurity," *Christian Science Monitor*, April 9, 2014

Jon Lindsay
"International Cyberwar Treaty Would Quickly Be Hacked to Bits," *U.S. News & World Report*, June 8, 2012.

Randolph May
"The Sony Hack Attack," Heartland Institute, December 26, 2014. www.heartland.org.

David M. Nicol
"Hacking the Lights Out: The Computer Virus Threat to the Electrical Grid," *Scientific American*, July 2011.

Nuala O'Connor
"Encryption Makes Us All Safer," Center for Democracy & Technology, October 8, 2014. www.cdt.org.

John Seabrook
"Network Insecurity," *New Yorker*, May 20, 2013.

Peter W. Singer
"The Cyber Terror Bogeyman," *Armed Forces Journal*, November 2012.

Marlisse Silver Sweeney
"What the Law Can (and Can't) Do About Online Harassment," *Atlantic*, November 12, 2014.

Jonathan M. Trugman — "How the US Is Losing the Escalating Cyberwar," *New York Post*, December 21, 2014.

Brandon Valeriano and Ryan Maness — "The Fog of Cyberwar: Why the Threat Doesn't Live Up to the Hype," *Foreign Affairs*, November 21, 2012.

John Villasenor — "The Two Classes of Cyber Threats," *Slate*, January 29, 2013. www.slate.com.

Ian Wallace — "Why the U.S. Is Not in a Cyber War," Daily Beast, March 10, 2013. www.thedailybeast.com.

Jody Westby — "Caution: Active Response to Cyber Attacks Has High Risk," *Forbes*, November 29, 2012.

Cathy Young — "Men Are Harassed More than Women Online," Daily Beast, September 4, 2014. www.thedailybeast.com.

Index

CPSIA information can be obtained
at www.ICGtesting.com
Printed in the USA
FFOW05n2222050116

9 780737 774214